WILLIAMS-SONOMA

weeknight
fresh + fast

Recipes and text **Kristine Kidd**

Photographs **Kate Sears**

weldon**owen**

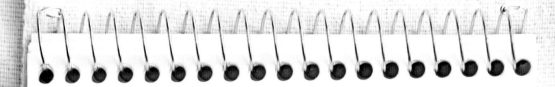

contents

what's for dinner tonight?

When you're as busy as I am, the answer to this daily question can sometimes be daunting. In this book, I'll show you just how effortless it is to create flavorful and nutritious meals—even on a busy schedule. The more than 100 delicious and beautifully photographed dinner ideas, organized by season, reflect my personal cooking philosophy: let the bounty of the season inspire your cooking. The fresh, full-flavored vegetables, fruit, and herbs I find at farmers' markets or quality produce displays need little help to shine, requiring only simple seasonings and straightforward cooking methods to make dinner brilliant. Whether you crave meat, poultry, fish, or a meatless dish, this book will show just how easy it is to put a satisfying and healthy dinner on the table in no time—no matter what the day brings!

Kristine Kidd

Finding inspiration from seasonal offerings helps spark my creativity. Every year I look forward to **spring** and the bright, fresh flavors it brings.

fresh & fast meals for **spring**

As winter draws to a close, I anticipate the verdant taste of the first slender asparagus shoots; the sweetness and crisp texture of snap peas; and the peppery punch of newly harvested radishes that mark the arrival of spring. The season brings with it some of the best types of vegetables for fast and fresh meals, as spring's bounty needs little preparation. Following are more than two dozen of my favorite seasonal recipes for quick sautés, easy stir-fries, hands-off roasts, and much more, which will enliven your spring suppers.

spring market inspirations

- apricots
- arugula
- asparagus
- avocadoes
- baby broccoli
- baby carrots
- bok choy
- broccoli rabe
- cherries
- cucumbers
- endive
- fennel
- green onions
- kale
- leeks
- morel mushrooms
- savoy cabbage
- strawberries
- sugar snap peas
- swiss chard
- radishes
- young potatoes

add a simple side

- Toss mixed baby lettuces with radishes, toasted nuts, and a bold-flavored cheese, such as feta, blue, or Parmesan

- Steam asparagus, baby broccoli, or sugar snap peas until tender, 3–7 minutes, and toss with a tangy vinaigrette

- Roast young potatoes with olive oil, salt, and pepper in a 425°F (220°C) oven until golden, 30–45 minutes

- Sauté young greens such as chard, kale, or broccoli rabe briefly in olive oil, then add chicken or vegetable broth; cover and simmer until tender, 5–10 minutes

choose fruit for dessert

- Sauté halved cherries with butter, brown sugar, and a little lemon juice until the fruit is soft, about 5 minutes; serve over vanilla frozen yogurt or ice cream

- In parfait glasses, alternate layers of apricot wedges with sugar, plain or vanilla-flavored Greek yogurt, and chopped toasted almonds

- Serve sliced fresh strawberries over pieces of purchased nut cake and top with thick Greek yogurt or crème fraiche

smart strategies for spring meals

start fresh I find that spring is the ideal time to clean out the pantry. First, remove everything and wipe the pantry clean. Next, discard any items that have passed their expiration date, or that you don't recall purchasing. Finally, restock with often-used staples like whole-grain pasta, canned beans and tomatoes, and spices (for more information on stocking the pantry, see page 225).

spice it up Spring meals in my house are simple, requiring just a few potent, all-purpose seasonings, such as mustard, cumin, and fennel seeds; chili powder; and red pepper flakes. Versatile staples in my cooking throughout the year, these spices will last for up to 12 months in a cool, dark place.

plant a kitchen garden With the brighter days, spring is the perfect time to plant an herb garden—either on a sunny windowsill or in the backyard—so that you can snip fresh herbs whenever you need them. Well maintained, the herbs should last well into the fall months.

tips for sautéing Many of the recipes in this chapter call for sautéing. For best results, select a pan that holds the food comfortably with a little extra space. If the pan is too small, the liquid will collect rather than evaporate and the food will steam rather than sear. If the pan is too large, the oil will tend to smoke and burn.

stay organized As you plan your weekly meals, check the contents of the refrigerator to determine what ingredients should be used that week. Aim to eat leftovers within a day or two.

Slender potatoes and asparagus make smart partners for spice-rubbed roasted chicken pieces. The entire meal cooks together, so there is no need for sides. Finish with fresh berries topped with sweetened yogurt mixed with lime zest.

spice-scented **roast chicken** and vegetables

Chicken, 1
(2¾–3 lb/1.35–1.5 kg),
cut into 8 pieces

Olive oil, 4 tablespoons
(2 fl oz/60 ml)

Low-sodium soy sauce,
1 tablespoon

Mustard seeds, 1 tablespoon

Cumin seeds, 1 tablespoon

Onion, 1, finely chopped

**Coarse kosher salt and
freshly ground pepper**

**Fingerling potatoes or
small red potatoes,** 1–1¼ lb
(500–625 g), halved
lengthwise

Asparagus, 2 bunches
(about 1 lb/500 g total),
ends trimmed

makes 4 servings

● Position one rack in the center of the oven, and one rack in the lower third of the oven and preheat to 425°F (220°C). Pat the chicken dry, and place in a large bowl; add 2 tablespoons of the oil and the soy sauce and toss to coat. In a spice grinder or mortar with pestle, grind the mustard seeds and cumin seeds. Set aside 2 teaspoons of the mixture; add the remaining mixture to the chicken. Add the onion, sprinkle with salt and pepper, and toss to coat. Arrange the chicken, skin side up, on ½ of a large rimmed baking sheet.

● Place the potatoes in the same bowl. Add 1 tablespoon of the oil, and toss to coat. Add the reserved 2 teaspoons spices, salt, and pepper, and toss to coat. Arrange the potatoes, cut side down, on the second half of the baking sheet. Place the baking sheet on the center rack in the oven and bake until the chicken legs, thighs, and wings start to brown and the breasts and potatoes are cooked through, about 40 minutes.

● Meanwhile, place the asparagus on a small rimmed baking sheet or pizza pan. Drizzle the spears with the remaining 1 tablespoon oil and toss to coat. Sprinkle lightly with salt and pepper.

● Transfer the chicken breasts and the potatoes to a warmed platter and tent with foil to keep warm. Place the asparagus on the lower oven rack. Roast the chicken and asparagus until the chicken legs, thighs, and wings are opaque when tested with a small paring knife and the asparagus is just tender-crisp, about 10 minutes. Add the asparagus and chicken to the platter and serve right away.

Sustainable wild Alaskan king salmon, an all-time favorite of mine, starts its season in early spring. A salad of mixed baby lettuce makes a vivid and light accompaniment. Smashed young potatoes would round out the meal perfectly.

roasted salmon with thyme vinaigrette

Dijon mustard, ½ tablespoon

Champagne vinegar or white wine vinegar, 2 teaspoons

Extra-virgin olive oil, 2½ tablespoons, plus more as needed

Shallot, 1 tablespoon minced

Fresh thyme, 2 teaspoons minced

Coarse kosher salt and freshly ground pepper

Salmon fillet, 1 (about ¾ lb/375 g)

Mixed baby lettuces, 3 cups (3 oz/90 g)

makes 2 servings

● Preheat the oven to 425°F (220°C). In a small bowl, place the mustard. Whisk in the vinegar. Gradually whisk in 2½ tablespoons oil. Mix in the shallot and thyme. Season the vinaigrette to taste with salt and pepper. Brush a small baking dish with oil. Place the salmon in the dish, skin side down. Spoon ½ of the vinaigrette over the salmon. Let marinate for 15–20 minutes at room temperature, or refrigerate for up to 1 hour.

● Roast the salmon until almost cooked through, about 15 minutes. Let it rest while preparing the salad.

● In a bowl, toss the lettuces with the remaining vinaigrette. Divide the salad between 2 plates. Cut the salmon in half and put one piece alongside the salad on each plate. Serve right away.

quick tips

The recipe easily doubles to serve four, or provides leftovers for a salmon salad dinner the next night. For convenience, make the vinaigrette a day ahead of time. You can also double or triple the dressing to have extra to use on salads later in the week.

A creamy risotto is a great way to feature fresh vegetables and herbs. Here, I've used sugar snap peas, leeks, and tarragon. Round out the meal with a green salad with radishes and end with strawberries splashed with balsamic vinegar.

risotto with leeks and sugar snaps

Low-sodium chicken or vegetable broth, 5½ cups (44 fl oz/1.35 l)

Sugar snap peas, 1 lb (500 g), strings removed

Olive oil, 1 tablespoon

Pancetta, 3 oz (90 g), minced

Leeks, 2, white and light green parts halved lengthwise and sliced crosswise

Arborio rice, 1½ cups (10½ oz/330 g)

Dry white wine, ½ cup (4 fl oz/125 ml)

Parmesan cheese, 1 cup (¼ lb/125 g) freshly grated

Fresh tarragon, 1 tablespoon minced

Coarse kosher salt and freshly ground pepper

makes 4 servings

In a saucepan, bring the broth to a boil. Add the sugar snap peas and cook until just tender-crisp, about 2 minutes. Using a slotted spoon, transfer the sugar snap peas to a bowl and set aside. Reduce the heat to low.

In a heavy saucepan over medium heat, warm the oil. Add the pancetta and stir until fragrant, about 1 minute. Add the leeks and cook until tender, stirring frequently, about 5 minutes. Add the rice and stir until opaque, about 1 minute. Add the wine and stir until absorbed. Add about ¾ cup (6 fl oz/180 ml) of the hot broth; adjust the heat so the liquid bubbles and is absorbed slowly. Cook, stirring frequently, until the liquid is absorbed. Continue cooking, adding the liquid about ¾ cup at a time and stirring frequently, until the rice is just tender but slightly firm in the center and the mixture is creamy, about 20 minutes.

Mix in the sugar snap peas, Parmesan, tarragon, and a generous amount of pepper. Taste and adjust the seasoning. Serve right away.

quick tips

Turn the leftovers into risotto cakes: For 3–4 cups (15–20 oz/470–630 g) of risotto, mix in 1 egg yolk and ⅓ cup panko (Japanese bread crumbs). Using wet hands, form the mixture into 2-inch (5-cm) balls, then flatten into rounds ¾ inch (2 cm) thick. Dip the cakes into beaten egg and coat with more panko, then brown in olive oil, about 4 minutes per side.

Here, thinly sliced steak enhanced with mustard seeds and peppercorns is served on a bed of arugula. The sauce is made from the pan juices enriched by a little balsamic vinegar. Round out the meal with country-style bread.

mustard-peppercorn **steak and arugula salad**

Peppercorns, 2 teaspoons

Mustard seeds, 1 teaspoon

Fresh rosemary,
1 tablespoon minced

Coarse kosher salt,
2 teaspoons

Top sirloin steak, 1¼ lb
(625 g), about 1 inch
(2.5 cm) thick

Olive oil

Balsamic vinegar,
½ cup (4 fl oz/125 ml)

Shallots, ¼ cup
(1½ oz/45 g) minced

Brown sugar, 1 teaspoon
firmly packed

Arugula, 6 cups (6 oz/185 g)

Red onion, ¼, thinly sliced

Radishes, ½ bunch,
thinly sliced

Lemon, ½

makes 4 servings

● In a spice mill or mortar with pestle, coarsely grind the peppercorns and mustard seeds. Transfer the mixture to a small bowl; stir in the rosemary and salt. Pat the steak dry, and then press the spice mixture into both sides.

● Brush a heavy, large frying pan with oil and place over high heat. Add the steak and cook as desired, about 4 minutes on each side for medium-rare. Transfer the steak to a work surface. Add the vinegar, shallots, and sugar to the frying pan and boil, stirring occasionally, until reduced to a glaze, about 1 minute. Transfer the glaze to a small bowl.

● Divide the arugula among 4 warmed plates and top with the red onion and radishes. Squeeze lemon juice over each. Slice the steak thin on an angle. Arrange the steak atop the arugula. Drizzle with the glaze and serve right away.

quick tips

Top sirloin is an economical and great-tasting cut of beef, and is perfect for weeknight cooking. Be certain to slice the meat thinly, or it may seem tough. The leftover steak is delicious in sandwiches.

Shrimp, endive, and lemon, quickly sautéed, make a novel topping for pasta, but the crisp herbed-infused crumbs give it an extra-special touch. The combination of fresh seafood, vegetables, and grain are a perfect one-dish meal.

linguine, shrimp, and endive with bread crumbs

Whole-grain or sourdough bread, 2 slices

Olive oil, 4 tablespoons (2 fl oz/60 ml)

Large shallot, 1, minced

Fresh thyme, 1 tablespoon, plus 2 teaspoons minced

Coarse kosher salt and freshly ground black pepper

Dried linguine, ¾–1 lb (375–500 g)

Large onion, 1, finely chopped

Red pepper flakes, ½ teaspoon

Fresh rosemary, 2 teaspoons minced

Large shrimp, 1 lb (500 g), peeled and deveined

Endive, 4 heads, cut in half lengthwise, and then cut crosswise into ½-inch (12-mm) slices

Fresh lemon juice, 3 tablespoons

Fresh flat-leaf parsley, finely chopped

makes 4 servings

● Tear the bread into 1-inch (2.5-cm) pieces. Place in a food processor and grind to fine crumbs. Measure 1½ cups (3 oz/90 g) of the crumbs to use in the recipe. In a large nonstick frying pan over medium-high heat, warm 2 tablespoons of the oil. Add the shallot and stir until fragrant, about 30 seconds. Add 1 tablespoon of the thyme and then the bread crumbs. Stir until the crumbs are crisp, about 3 minutes. Season to taste with salt and black pepper. Transfer the crumb mixture to a small bowl and set aside.

● Bring a large pot three-fourths full of salted water to a boil. Add the pasta, stir well, and cook until al dente, about 10 minutes.

● Meanwhile, wipe out the same frying pan. Set the frying pan over medium heat, and warm the remaining 2 tablespoons of the oil. Add the onion, pepper flakes, and rosemary. Sauté until the onion begins to soften, about 5 minutes. Add the shrimp, sprinkle with salt and pepper, and cook on the first side until they begin to color, about 2 minutes. Turn the shrimp over; add the endive and the remaining 2 teaspoons of the thyme. Sauté until the shrimp are cooked through and the endive starts to soften, about 4 minutes. Add the lemon juice and boil until almost evaporated, about 30 seconds. Remove the frying pan from the heat.

● Remove 1 cup (8 fl oz/250 ml) of the pasta cooking liquid, and reserve. Drain the pasta, and then transfer to a warmed large, shallow bowl. Add the shrimp mixture and ½ cup (4 fl oz/125 ml) of the pasta cooking liquid; toss to coat the pasta, adding more pasta cooking liquid as needed to moisten. Taste the dish and adjust the seasoning.

● Sprinkle the pasta with the herbed bread crumbs. Garnish with the chopped parsley and serve right away.

Peppery radishes and refreshing mint deliver bright spring flavors to healthful chicken breasts. A quick side dish of lentils dressed in the same vinaigrette that sauces the chicken makes this a complete, protein-rich meal.

chicken breasts with lentil-radish-mint salad

Brown lentils, 1 cup (7 oz/220 g), picked over and rinsed

Small red onion, 1, cut in half

Bay leaf, 1

Coarse kosher salt

Red wine vinegar, 2 tablespoons plus 1 teaspoon

Large celery ribs, 2, finely chopped

Radishes, 1 large bunch, trimmed, quartered lengthwise, and sliced

Fresh mint, 7 tablespoons (⅔ oz/20 g) minced

Dijon mustard, 3 tablespoons

Extra-virgin olive oil, ½ cup (4 fl oz/125 ml), plus 2 tablespoons

Freshly ground pepper

Skinless, boneless chicken breast halves, 4 (about 6 oz/185 g each)

All-purpose flour for dredging

makes 4 servings

In a saucepan, place the lentils; add enough water to cover by 2 inches (5 cm). Add ½ of the onion and the bay leaf, and bring to a boil. Reduce the heat, cover partially, and simmer until the lentils are just tender, about 30 minutes. Remove from the heat and stir in 2 teaspoons salt and 1 teaspoon vinegar. Drain the lentils and transfer to a medium bowl, remove and discard the ½ onion and bay leaf. Finely chop the remaining ½ of the onion. Mix the onion, celery, radishes, and 3 tablespoons of the mint into the lentils. Set aside.

In a small bowl, place the mustard. Whisk in the remaining 2 tablespoons vinegar. Gradually whisk in ½ cup (4 fl oz/125 ml) of the oil. Mix in the remaining 4 tablespoons (⅓ oz/10 g) of the mint. Season the dressing with salt and pepper. Set aside 3 tablespoons dressing to use as sauce. Mix enough of the remaining dressing into the salad and season to taste.

Working with 1 chicken breast half at a time, place on a sheet of waxed paper, and cover with a second sheet of waxed paper. Using a rolling pin, hit the chicken a few times to flatten slightly to an even thickness. Transfer the chicken to a plate and sprinkle with salt and pepper. Spread the flour on another plate. Dredge the chicken in the flour, shaking off any excess. In 2 large nonstick frying pans over medium-high heat, warm 1 tablespoon oil in each. Add 2 chicken breast halves to each pan. Sauté the chicken until cooked through, 4–5 minutes per side.

Slice the chicken, transfer the chicken to warmed plates, and spoon the lentil salad alongside. Drizzle the chicken with the reserved dressing and serve.

quick tips

The salad can be made one day ahead and chilled, or you can double it and serve the leftovers the next night. If you are cooking for two, make the entire recipe and use the leftover chicken in sandwiches.

Young cabbage lightens the texture of mashed potatoes and gives them a new flavor component in this meal-in-one recipe. For easy slicing, freeze the meat for about 30 minutes before cutting. Leftover meat makes great sandwiches.

beef medallions with spring mashed potatoes

Yukon gold potatoes, 1½ lb (750 g), peeled and cut into 1-inch (2.5-cm) pieces

Coarse kosher salt and freshly ground pepper

Olive oil, 3 tablespoons

Small savoy cabbage, ½ head, cored and thinly sliced crosswise

Unsalted butter, 1–2 tablespoons

Beef tri-tip roast, 1¼ lb (625 g), excess fat trimmed

Large shallots, 2, halved lengthwise and thinly sliced crosswise

All-purpose flour, 1 tablespoon

Low-sodium beef broth, 2 cups (16 fl oz/500 ml)

Dry vermouth, 2 tablespoons

Dijon mustard, 2 teaspoons

Fresh thyme, 1½ tablespoons minced, plus more for garnish

makes 4 servings

In a large pot, put the potatoes. Add enough water to cover by 2 inches (5 cm), and then add 1 teaspoon kosher salt. Bring to a boil and cook until the potatoes are tender, about 10 minutes.

Meanwhile, in a large nonstick frying pan over medium heat, warm 1 tablespoon of the oil. Add the cabbage, and season with salt and pepper. Sauté until almost tender, about 8 minutes. Set aside.

Using a ladle, remove 1 cup (8 fl oz/250 ml) potato cooking liquid and reserve. Drain the potatoes. Return the potatoes to the same pot and mash coarsely with a fork, thinning with the cooking liquid as needed. Mix in 1 tablespoon butter, the cabbage and a generous amount of pepper. Taste and adjust the seasoning if needed. Cover to keep warm.

Working across the grain, cut the beef into ¼-inch (6-mm) slices, and then cut the slices into 2-inch (5-cm) lengths. In a large frying pan over medium-high heat, warm 1 tablespoon of the oil. Working in batches, add the beef in a single layer and cook until just colored, about 30 seconds per side. Transfer the beef to a plate and season with salt and pepper.

Add the remaining 1 tablespoon oil to the frying pan. Add the shallots, reduce the heat to medium, and stir until tender and golden brown, about 6 minutes. Add the flour and stir for 20 seconds to remove the raw flavor. Gradually mix in the beef broth and vermouth. Simmer until the sauce thickens slightly, stirring frequently, about 6 minutes. Stir in the mustard and 1½ tablespoons thyme. Remove the frying pan from the heat, add 1 tablespoon butter, if desired, and stir until melted. Taste and adjust the seasoning if needed.

Transfer the beef and potatoes to a platter or divide among 4 warmed plates. Drizzle the sauce over the beef, sprinkle with minced thyme, and serve right away.

25

Asparagus and goat cheese are an inventive topping for pizza. For a real treat, use well-drained buffalo milk mozzarella in place of cow's milk cheese. Round out the meal with a lemon-dressed romaine and cucumber salad.

pizza with pancetta, asparagus, and goat cheese

Olive oil, 2 tablespoons

Pancetta, 2 oz (60 g), minced

Red pepper flakes,
¼ teaspoon

Slender asparagus, 1 bunch
(about ½ lb/250 g), ends
trimmed

Pizza dough (see tips),
1 lb (500 g)

Cornmeal

**Whole-milk mozzarella
cheese,** 6 oz (185 g), shredded

Green onions, 4, white and
pale green parts thinly sliced

Soft, fresh goat cheese,
¼ lb (125 g) crumbled

Parmesan cheese

**Coarse kosher salt
and freshly ground
black pepper**

makes 4 servings

● Preheat the oven to 450°F (230°C). In a frying pan over medium heat, warm 1 tablespoon of the oil. Add the pancetta and pepper flakes. Sauté until the pancetta browns, about 2 minutes. Remove from the heat. Cut each asparagus spear into 3 pieces, and then cut the thick ends in half lengthwise. Place the asparagus in a small bowl; add the remaining 1 tablespoon oil and toss to coat.

● Roll out the pizza dough on a lightly floured surface to an 11- to 12-inch (28- to 30-cm) oval or round. Sprinkle a rimless baking sheet with cornmeal; transfer the pizza dough to the pan. Brush the dough with the pancetta-cooking oil, and sprinkle with the pancetta mixture. Spread the mozzarella cheese over the dough, leaving a ½-inch (12-mm) plain edge. Sprinkle the green onions and then the goat cheese over the mozzarella. Arrange the asparagus over the pizza. Grate some Parmesan cheese over the asparagus, then season with salt and pepper.

● Place the pizza in the oven and bake until the asparagus is tender and the edges of the crust are brown, about 20 minutes. Transfer the pizza to a cutting board. Let stand 5 minutes. Cut into small pieces or wedges and serve.

quick tips

For convenience, this recipe uses prepared pizza dough, but if you have a bit more time, you can use the recipe on page 232. Look for fresh dough at a specialty-food market or natural food store. It will be fresher and use healthier ingredients than the dough sold in tubes. Chopped pancetta can be found in the packaged deli section of some markets.

Plain yogurt flavored with green onions, ginger, and cilantro makes a bright and simple sauce for mild-flavored tilapia. Serve with saffron-infused rice and broccoli tossed with olive oil, ground cumin, salt, and pepper.

sautéed tilapia with green onion–ginger raita

Plain yogurt, ⅔ cup
(5 oz/155 g)

Olive oil, 3 tablespoons,
plus more as needed

Green onions, 4, white
and pale green parts minced

Fresh ginger, 2 teaspoons
peeled and minced

Fresh cilantro, 2 tablespoons
minced, plus leaves for
garnish

**Coarse kosher salt and
freshly ground pepper**

Tilapia fillets, 4 (about
6 oz/185 g each)

Madras curry powder,
2 teaspoons

makes 4 servings

● In a bowl, place the yogurt and set aside. In a nonstick frying pan over medium heat, warm 2 tablespoons of the oil. Add the green onions and ginger and sauté until fragrant, about 30 seconds. Add to the yogurt. Add the cilantro, and mix to blend. Season the raita to taste with salt and pepper. Set aside.

● Sprinkle the fish fillets on both sides with the curry powder, salt, and pepper. In a large nonstick frying pan over medium-high heat, warm the remaining 1 tablespoon oil. Add the fish fillets and sauté until they are just cooked through, 2–3 minutes on each side.

● Transfer the fish to warmed plates and serve right away with the raita.

quick tips

Tilapia is an environmentally sound fish choice; this dish would be equally delicious with trout, Arctic char, or salmon, which are also sustainable. The versatile raita can be made a day ahead and chilled. It is also delicious as a sauce for chicken or as a dressing for potato salad.

A cherry tomato salsa brings a bright flavor to this quick dish. Round out the meal with a salad of baby lettuce, radishes, and red onion. For a special treat, replace the creminis with wild mushrooms such as chanterelles or morels.

mushroom and manchego **quesadillas**

Serrano chiles, 1½

Cherry tomatoes or pear tomatoes, ⅔ cup (3 oz/90 g), quartered

Fresh cilantro, 2 tablespoons minced

Green onion, 1, white and green parts thinly sliced

Coarse kosher salt and freshly ground pepper

Olive oil, 2 tablespoons

Large shallots, 2, minced

Cremini mushrooms, 10 oz (315 g), sliced

Small corn tortillas, 6

Manchego cheese, 5 oz (155 g), shredded (about 1½ cups)

makes 2 servings

● Seed and chop the whole chile and set aside. Seed and mince the remaining ½ chile. Mix the tomatoes, cilantro, green onion, and minced chile in a small bowl. Season the salsa to taste with salt and pepper. Set aside.

● In a large nonstick frying pan over medium-high heat, warm the oil. Add the shallots and stir until fragrant, about 1 minute. Add the mushrooms and chopped chile; sprinkle with salt and pepper. Sauté until the juices evaporate, about 5 minutes. Taste and adjust the seasoning.

● Heat a griddle or large frying pan over medium-low heat. Add 2 tortillas and cook until softened slightly, about 30 seconds. Turn the tortillas over. Spread ¼ cup (1 oz/30 g) of the cheese over ½ of each tortilla, leaving a border around the edges. Spread ¼ cup of the mushroom mixture over the cheese on each. Fold the empty side of the tortillas over the filling and press lightly. Cook until light golden and crisp, about 3 minutes on each side. Transfer to warmed plates. Repeat with the remaining tortillas, cheese, and mushroom mixture, adding more tortillas to the griddle after folding the quesadillas in half.

● Divide the quesadillas between warmed plates. Serve right away with the salsa.

quick tips

This dish can easily be doubled, but you will need to cook the quesadillas in several batches. Keep the first batch warm in a preheated 200°F (95°C) oven while cooking the remaining batches.

Here, chicken and vegetables are cooked in a clear, spice-infused broth. Served with herbs and bean sprouts, it is a refreshing one-dish meal. I like to nibble on sliced cucumbers sprinkled with salt and fresh mint while simmering the soup.

asian-style **chicken soup** with baby bok choy

Low-sodium chicken broth, 8 cups (64 fl oz/2 l)

Green onions, 1 bunch, white and green parts, plus green parts, thinly sliced, for serving

Fresh ginger, 2-inch (5-cm) piece, peeled and sliced

Asian fish sauce, 2 tablespoons

Sugar, 1 tablespoon

Star anise pods, 6

Cloves, 6

Skinless, boneless chicken breasts, 1–1¼ lb (500–625 g)

Thai chiles, 3, or 1 serrano chile, thinly sliced

Bean sprouts, fresh basil sprigs, fresh cilantro sprigs, and lime wedges for serving

Hoisin sauce (optional)

Baby bok choy, 4

Dried rice stick noodles (maifun), 6–7 oz (185–220 g)

Coarse kosher salt and freshly ground pepper

makes 4 servings

- In a large pot over high heat, combine the broth and 2 cups (16 fl oz/500 ml) water. Cut the green onion bunch in half crosswise and add to the pot; add the ginger, fish sauce, and sugar. In a tea ball, combine the star anise and cloves; add to the pot. Bring the broth to a boil. Add the chicken breasts, return to a boil, reduce the heat to medium-low, and simmer until the chicken is cooked through, 10–15 minutes, depending on the size of the chicken. Using tongs, transfer the chicken to a plate and set aside until ready to use. Simmer the broth to develop flavor, 15–30 minutes.

- Place the sliced green onions, sliced chiles, bean sprouts, herb sprigs, lime wedges, and hoisin sauce, if using, on a platter or in small bowls and set out on the table.

- Slice the bok choy crosswise about ½ inch thick. Thinly slice the chicken breasts crosswise. In a large bowl, place the noodles. Cover the noodles with very hot water and let soak for 3 minutes.

- Using tongs, remove the green onions and ginger from the pot and discard. Season the broth to taste with salt and pepper. Add the baby bok choy to the pot, raise the heat to high, and bring to a boil. Drain the noodles, add to the broth, and cook until just tender, about 2 minutes.

- Using tongs, divide the noodles and bok choy among 4 warmed deep bowls. Divide the chicken among the bowls. Ladle the broth over the top. Serve right away, allowing diners to add the condiments to taste.

Somehow, the fresh, tangy taste of fresh goat cheese just reminds me of spring. Here, it enhances a deceptively easy herb-flecked soufflé accented by tarragon, thyme, and lemon. Serve it with a butter lettuce salad and slices of rustic bread.

goat cheese soufflé with fresh herbs

Unsalted butter for greasing

Freshly grated Parmesan cheese or dried bread crumbs

Extra-virgin olive oil, ¼ cup (2 fl oz/60 ml)

Large shallots, 2, minced

All-purpose flour, 5 tablespoons (1½ oz/45 g)

Whole milk, 1¼ cups (10 fl oz/310 ml)

Dry white wine, ¼ cup (2 fl oz/60 ml)

Large eggs, 6

Large egg whites, 2

Coarse kosher salt, 1 teaspoon

Fresh lemon thyme or thyme, 1 tablespoon minced

Fresh tarragon, 2½ teaspoons minced

Soft fresh goat cheese, 1½ cups (½ lb/250 g) crumbled

Freshly ground pepper

makes 4 servings

● Preheat the oven to 400°F (200°C). Generously butter a 10-cup (2.5-l) soufflé dish or 12-cup (3-l) high-sided casserole. Sprinkle with Parmesan cheese. In a heavy large saucepan over medium heat, warm the oil. Add the shallots and sauté until tender, about 2 minutes. Add the flour and stir until the mixture bubbles, about 1 minute. Gradually whisk in the milk, then the wine. Cook, whisking constantly, until smooth, thickened, and beginning to boil, about 2 minutes. Remove from the heat.

● Separate the 6 whole eggs, placing the yolks in a medium bowl and the whites in a large bowl or the bowl of a stand mixer. Add the 2 egg whites to the bowl with the other whites. Gradually whisk about ¼ of the hot milk mixture into the yolks, and then whisk the mixture back into the remaining milk mixture. Mix in the salt, herbs, cheese, and a generous amount of pepper.

● Using an electric mixer, beat the whites until stiff but not dry. Fold ¼ of the whites into the lukewarm cheese mixture to lighten. Fold in the remaining whites. Transfer the mixture to the prepared dish.

● Place the soufflé dish in the oven and reduce the oven heat to 375°F (190°C). Bake until the soufflé is golden, puffed, and gently set in the center, about 35 minutes. Serve right away.

quick tips

To easily separate the egg yolks from the whites, crack all the eggs into one bowl, and then gently lift out the yolks, allowing the whites to flow through your fingers back into the bowl. The soufflé can be assembled 1 hour ahead of time; cover and let stand at room temperature before baking.

I love how Thai-style ingredients make this salad vivid and light. Here, I've paired them with quickly marinated and briefly sautéed beef. Serve with fresh spring rolls purchased from an Asian restaurant or specialty-food store.

seared beef salad with thai flavors

Beef top sirloin, 1 lb (500 g), fat trimmed, cut in half lengthwise

Fresh lemongrass, 2 tablespoons minced from bottom 6 inches (15 cm) of the stalk

Asian fish sauce, 2 tablespoons

Low-sodium soy sauce, 1 tablespoon

Sugar, 1½ teaspoons

Large shallots, 2, minced

Freshly ground pepper

Peanut oil, 4 tablespoons (2 fl oz/60 ml)

Fresh lime juice, 3 tablespoons

Serrano chiles, 1½–2, seeded and minced

Coarse kosher salt

Red leaf lettuce, 1 head, torn into bite-size pieces

Bean sprouts, ¾ lb (375 g)

Persian cucumbers, 4, halved lengthwise, and then sliced crosswise

Fresh basil leaves, preferably Thai basil, 1 cup (30 g) packed

Fresh mint leaves, ⅓ cup (⅓ oz/10 g) packed

Red onion, ½, thinly sliced

makes 4 servings

● Freeze the beef for 30 minutes. Cut across the grain into ¼-inch (6-mm) slices. In a medium bowl, combine the lemongrass, 1 tablespoon of the fish sauce, the soy sauce, ¾ teaspoon of the sugar, ½ of the minced shallots, and a generous amount of pepper; stir to mix well. Add the beef, stir to coat, and let it marinate for 15–30 minutes at room temperature.

● Meanwhile, in a small bowl, combine 3 tablespoons of the oil, the lime juice, chiles, remaining 1 tablespoon fish sauce, the remaining ¾ teaspoon sugar, and the remaining shallots. Season the dressing with salt and pepper.

● In a large bowl, combine the lettuce, bean sprouts, cucumbers, basil, mint, and onion. Toss to mix. Add the dressing and toss to coat.

● In a heavy large frying pan over high heat, warm the remaining 1 tablespoon oil. Working in batches, add the beef in a single layer (do not crowd the frying pan) and cook until just brown, about 20 seconds on each side. Arrange the beef on top of the salad. Serve right away.

quick tips

Partially freezing the beef for about 30 minutes makes it easy to slice into thin pieces, which then cook quickly in a hot pan. To save time, you can make the dressing one day ahead and chill. Bring it to room temperature and mix well before using. If you can't find lemongrass, substitute 1 teaspoon finely grated lemon zest.

Spaghetti carbonara, the egg-rich pasta dish from Rome, is one of my all-time favorite dinners. My creative take includes healthful and tasty spring greens. In Italian fashion, I like to complete the meal with biscotti and fresh fruit.

spaghetti carbonara with black kale

Pancetta, 3 oz (90 g), chopped

Large shallot, 1, minced

Dry white wine, ¼ cup (2 fl oz/60 ml)

Dried spaghetti, 6–8 oz (185–250 g), preferably multigrain

Black kale or other hearty greens, 1 bunch, chopped

Large eggs, 2

Parmesan cheese, ½ cup (2 oz/60 g) freshly grated

Romano cheese, ¼ cup (1 oz/30 g) freshly grated

Freshly ground black pepper

makes 2 servings; can be doubled

● Place a large nonstick frying pan over medium-high heat. Add the pancetta and sauté until beginning to brown, about 3 minutes. Add the shallot and stir for 2 minutes. Add the wine and boil until reduced by half, stirring up the browned bits, about 30 seconds. Remove the frying pan from the heat.

● Bring a large pot three-fourths full of salted water to a boil. Add the spaghetti, stir well, and cook for 5 minutes. Add the kale and cook until the pasta is al dente, about 5 minutes longer.

● Meanwhile, in a small bowl, add the eggs and beat with a fork. Mix in both cheeses and a generous amount of pepper.

● Remove ½ cup (4 fl oz/125 ml) of the pasta cooking water and reserve. Drain the pasta. Reheat the pancetta mixture briefly, and then remove from the heat. Add the spaghetti and kale to the frying pan. Gradually whisk ¼ cup (2 fl oz/60 ml) of the reserved pasta cooking liquid into the egg mixture. Add the egg mixture to the frying pan and stir until it coats the pasta and is creamy, not wet and runny. If the egg mixture does not become creamy, set the frying pan over very low heat and stir constantly just until it becomes creamy, watching carefully (do not boil). Immediately remove the frying pan from the heat. Mix in enough of the remaining ¼ cup pasta cooking liquid to form a silky texture.

● Divide between 2 warmed bowls and serve right away.

quick tips

To prevent overcooking, which will cause curdling, take the frying pan off the heat before mixing in the egg mixture. Then, only if necessary, cook over very low heat and stir constantly just until the eggs start to thicken.

A whole chicken roasted with vegetables makes a comforting dinner. In this version, I flavor the bird with tarragon and thyme, and tuck tender spring potatoes and carrots alongside. Offer fresh apricots and cookies for dessert.

roast chicken with young potatoes and carrots

Chicken, 1 (4 lb/2 kg)

Fresh tarragon, 4 sprigs, 4 teaspoons minced, plus more for garnish

Fresh thyme, 4 sprigs, 4 teaspoons minced, plus more for garnish

Coarse kosher salt and freshly ground pepper

Young potatoes, 2 lb (1 kg), 1½–2 inches (4–5 cm) in diameter, cut in half

Carrots, 2 lb (1 kg), peeled, cut into 2-inch (5-cm) pieces

Olive oil, 2 tablespoons

Dry white wine, ½ cup (4 fl oz/125 ml)

makes 4 servings

● Preheat the oven to 450°F (230°C). Grease a heavy large rimmed baking sheet (not a roasting pan). Pull out and discard the fat and giblets from the main cavity in the chicken. Pat the chicken very dry with paper towels. Starting at the edge of the main cavity, slide a finger under the skin over each breast half, making pockets. Place 1 sprig tarragon and 1 sprig thyme in each pocket. Sprinkle the chicken with 1½ teaspoons each minced tarragon and thyme, and season with salt and pepper. Place the remaining 2 sprigs tarragon and 2 sprigs thyme into the main cavity. Place the chicken on the prepared sheet and roast for 30 minutes.

● Meanwhile, in a large bowl, place the potatoes and carrots. Add the olive oil and toss to coat. Add 2 teaspoons each minced tarragon and thyme. Sprinkle lightly with salt and pepper, and toss to coat.

● After the chicken has roasted for 30 minutes, remove it from the oven. Tilt the sheet and spoon off most of the fat. Arrange the chicken in the center of the pan and spoon the vegetables around the bird, turning the potatoes cut side down. Return the pan to the center of the oven and continue roasting until an instant-read thermometer inserted into the thickest part of a thigh registers 165°F (74°C), about 40 minutes longer. Transfer the potatoes and carrots to a warmed baking dish or platter. Using pot holders, lift the bird and tip it, letting the juices run into a heavy small saucepan. Transfer the chicken to the dish or platter to rest.

● Pour the juices from the baking sheet into a small bowl and degrease; add the juices to the saucepan. Add the wine to the baking sheet. Set the sheet over medium heat and bring the wine to a boil, stirring up any browned bits. Pour the wine into the saucepan. Boil until reduced slightly, about 5 minutes. Add any juices from the chicken platter. Mix the remaining ½ teaspoon each minced tarragon and thyme into the sauce. Taste and adjust the seasoning. Sprinkle the chicken, potatoes, and carrots with minced tarragon and thyme.

● Carve the chicken and serve right away with the potatoes, carrots, and sauce.

Greens, lemon, and tarragon make refreshing counterpoints to scallops' inherent richness. I like to spoon this creative and colorful dish over aromatic rice, so it can soak up the delicious sauce. Toasted pecans lend appealing crunch.

sautéed scallops and swiss chard

Olive oil, 3 tablespoons

Red or white chard, 1 small bunch, stems removed, leaves chopped

Coarse kosher salt and freshly ground pepper

Sea scallops, ¾ lb (375 g)

All-purpose flour for dredging

Small shallot, 1, minced

Dry white wine, ¼ cup (2 fl oz/60 ml)

Low-sodium chicken broth, ½ cup (4 fl oz/125 ml)

Fresh lemon juice, 1 tablespoon

Dijon mustard, ½ teaspoon

Fresh tarragon, ½ teaspoon minced, plus more for garnish

Unsalted butter, 1 tablespoon (optional)

Cooked brown jasmine or basmati rice

Pecans, 2 tablespoons toasted and chopped (optional)

makes 2 servings

● In a large nonstick frying pan over medium-high heat, warm 1 tablespoon of the oil. Add the chard and sprinkle lightly with salt and pepper. Sauté until just softened, about 3 minutes. Transfer to a bowl and cover to keep warm.

● Sprinkle the scallops lightly with salt and pepper, and then dredge in flour to coat. In the same frying pan over medium-high heat, warm 1 tablespoon of the oil. Add the scallops and cook until springy to the touch and no longer translucent in the center, about 3 minutes on each side. Using tongs, transfer the scallops to a plate. Add the remaining 1 tablespoon oil to the frying pan, and then add the shallot. Sauté until it begins to soften, about 1 minute. Add the wine and boil until almost evaporated, stirring up any browned bits, about 2 minutes. Add the chicken broth, lemon juice, mustard, and ½ teaspoon tarragon, and boil until slightly thickened, about 2 minutes. Remove from the heat, add the butter, if using, and stir until melted. Season the sauce to taste with salt and pepper.

● Spoon rice into the center of 2 warmed plates, and then spoon the chard over. Arrange the scallops atop the chard, and then spoon the sauce over all. Garnish with minced tarragon and pecans, if using, and serve right away.

quick tips

If you have other hearty spring greens or even broccoli rabe on hand, they can be substituted for the chard. Also, fresh thyme would work as well as tarragon. This recipe can be easily doubled to serve more.

Delicate savoy cabbage mixed with cilantro and lime juice makes a novel topping for a favorite family dish; fold it into the tortillas with the chicken and onions. Start off with purchased guacamole or salsa and chips.

chicken fajitas with savoy cabbage slaw

Olive oil, 4 tablespoons (2 fl oz/60 ml), plus more as needed

Chili powder, 2 teaspoons

Dried oregano, 1 teaspoon crumbled

Skinless, boneless chicken breasts, 1¼ lb (625 g)

Large red onions, 2, halved, sliced lengthwise

Coarse kosher salt and freshly ground pepper

Small flour tortillas or corn tortillas, about 6 inches (15 cm) in diameter, 8–12

Small savoy cabbage, ½ head, halved, cored, and thinly sliced

Fresh cilantro, ¼ cup (⅓ oz/10 g) chopped

Fresh lime juice, 2 tablespoons

Large avocado, 1, pitted, peeled, and sliced

makes 4 servings

● In a large bowl, combine 2 tablespoons of the oil, chili powder, and oregano. Cut the chicken crosswise into ½-inch (12-mm) slices, and then halve the large pieces lengthwise and crosswise. Add to the bowl with the seasonings. Add the onion and toss to coat. Sprinkle with salt and pepper. Let marinate while preparing the tortillas and cabbage.

● Preheat the oven to 350°F (180°C). Wrap the tortillas in foil and place in the oven until heated through, about 15 minutes.

● In another large bowl, combine the cabbage and cilantro. Add the remaining 2 tablespoons of oil and toss to coat. Add the lime juice and toss well. Season the cabbage to taste with salt and pepper. Transfer the cabbage to a serving bowl. Arrange the avocado slices in a small bowl.

● Place 1 large griddle over 2 burners, or 2 small griddles or 2 large frying pans over separate burners, and then heat over medium-high heat; brush with oil. Spread the chicken and onions on the griddle or pans. Cook, turning occasionally with tongs, until the chicken is cooked through, about 5 minutes, and the onions are brown, about 7 minutes.

● Transfer the chicken and onions to a warmed platter. Serve with the warm tortillas, cabbage mixture, and avocados, allowing diners to fill tortillas with chicken and onions, then cabbage and avocados.

quick tips

The cabbage slaw can be made one day ahead of time. If you have it on hand, you can replace the chicken with skirt steak, flank steak, or mahi mahi. Leftovers can be easily reheated and enjoyed again another night.

Cooking greens are abundant in spring. Tuscan kale (also know as black kale) is a personal favorite and is used here to add freshness to pasta. Fresh ricotta makes a satisfyingly easy sauce; look for it at Italian delis and upscale markets.

penne with ricotta cheese and greens

Tuscan kale or other hearty greens, 1 bunch, thick stems trimmed, cut crosswise into 2-inch (5-cm) pieces

Dried penne, preferably multigrain, 6–8 oz (185–250 g)

Extra-virgin olive oil, 2 tablespoons

Fresh thyme, 2 teaspoons minced

Shallot, 1, minced

Lemon zest, 1 teaspoon grated

Parmesan cheese, ½ cup (2 oz/60 g) freshly grated

Fresh whole-milk ricotta cheese, ½ cup (¼ lb/125 g)

Coarse kosher salt and freshly ground pepper

makes 2 servings

● Bring a large pot three-fourths full of salted water to a boil. Add the kale or other greens. Boil until the greens are just tender, 30 seconds to 6 minutes, depending on the variety of greens. Using a skimmer or slotted spoon, transfer the kale to a colander and drain. Return the water in the pot to a boil, add the pasta, stir well, and cook until al dente, about 10 minutes.

● Scoop out 1 cup (8 fl oz/250 ml) of pasta cooking water and reserve. Drain the pasta in the same colander with the greens. Return the pasta to the pot, press on the greens to remove some of the excess water, and add to the pot. Add the oil, thyme, shallot, and lemon zest, and toss to coat. Mix in the Parmesan and ricotta cheeses. If the mixture is dry, add enough of the reserved pasta cooking water to moisten. Season to taste with salt and pepper.

● Divide between warmed plates and serve right away.

quick tips

Here's another recipe that can be easily doubled. Cooking the greens in the pasta water adds a touch of flavor and saves you from washing another pot. Avoid using mass-marketed ricotta cheese, as it has an inferior flavor and texture; you need the real thing for this sauce.

Here, I have supplemented an egg base with bread cubes to create a cross between a bread pudding and a frittata. Comté, a superior quality Gruyère-style cheese, adds rich flavor, making this a perfect light dinner for a family of four.

broccoli and comté **frittata**

Broccoli, 1 lb (500 g)

Olive oil, 2 tablespoons

Bread cubes, 1 cup (2 oz/60 g) finely diced, from coarse country white bread or baguette

Large eggs, 10

Fresh chives, ⅓ cup (½ oz/15 g) minced

Fresh marjoram, 2 tablespoons minced

Coarse kosher salt and freshly ground pepper

Comté or Gruyère cheese, 1⅓ cups (5 oz/155 g) coarsely shredded

Large shallots, 2, sliced and rings separated

makes 4 servings

● Cut the florets off the broccoli stems, and then cut into ½-inch (12-mm) pieces. Peel the broccoli stems, and then cut into ½-inch pieces. In a steamer over boiling water, steam the broccoli florets and stems until just tender-crisp, about 4 minutes. Transfer to a colander. In a 12-inch (30-cm) nonstick ovenproof frying pan over medium-high heat, warm 1 tablespoon of the oil. Add the bread cubes and sauté until golden brown, about 4 minutes. Transfer the bread to a plate.

● In a large bowl, combine the eggs, chives, marjoram, ¾ teaspoon salt, and a generous amount of black pepper. Beat with a fork to blend. Mix in 1 cup (4 oz/125 g) of the cheese.

● In the same frying pan over medium heat, warm the remaining 1 tablespoon oil. Add the shallots and sauté until golden brown, about 4 minutes. Add the broccoli, sprinkle with salt and pepper, and sauté until heated through, about 4 minutes. Mix the bread cubes into the egg mixture, and then pour the mixture into the frying pan. Gently stir to distribute evenly. Reduce the heat to medium-low, cover the frying pan, and cook until the eggs are almost set but still moist in the center, about 12 minutes.

● Preheat the broiler. Sprinkle the remaining ⅓ cup cheese over the frittata. Broil until the eggs puff, the center is springy to the touch, and the cheese begins to brown, about 3 minutes. Using a flexible spatula, loosen the frittata around the edges and slide the frittata onto a platter. Serve warm or at room temperature, cutting into wedges to serve.

quick tips

The frittata is large, and leftovers make great sandwich fillings. Or, you can cut the remaining frittata into small pieces and serve at room temperature as a starter for the next evening's meal.

Mint and lamb are traditional in spring. I like to combine them in an unusual and delicious way, making an Italian-style salsa verde. Serve with steamed potatoes and asparagus, which are also delightful dipped into the salsa.

lamb chops with mint salsa verde

Fresh mint leaves, ½ cup
(½ oz/15 g) lightly packed

Fresh flat-leaf parsley leaves,
½ cup (½ oz/15 g) lightly
packed

Small shallot, 1, coarsely
chopped

Coarse kosher salt,
¼ teaspoon

Red pepper flakes

Extra-virgin olive oil,
¼ cup (2 fl oz/60 ml)

Fresh lemon juice,
1½ teaspoons

Freshly ground black pepper

**Lamb shoulder round
bone chops,** 4, each 1 inch
(2.5 cm) thick

makes 4 servings

● To make the salsa verde, in a food processor, combine the mint, parsley, shallot, salt, and a pinch of red pepper flakes. Pulse, using on-off turns, until a coarse paste forms. With the machine running, gradually pour in 3 tablespoons of the oil, then the lemon juice. Mix in a generous amount of black pepper.

● Sprinkle the lamb with salt and pepper. In a heavy large frying pan over medium-high heat, warm the remaining 1 tablespoon olive oil. Add the lamb to the frying pan and cook to the desired doneness, about 3 minutes per side for medium-rare. Transfer the lamb to warmed plates. Spoon a little of the salsa verde on top of each chop and serve right away.

quick tips

Make extra salsa verde and store it in the refrigerator to accompany chicken, fish, or potatoes. The sauce is thick and intense, but it can be thinned to the desired texture with more olive oil.

Lemon and fresh herbs are a smart complement to mild fish. Here, I've used them in a crunchy bread crumb topping. When wild mushrooms are in season, sauté them and serve them on top. Offer green beans and rice on the side.

black cod with lemon and thyme bread crumbs

Olive oil, 2 teaspoons, plus more as needed

Black cod or arctic char fillets, 4 (about 6 oz/185 g each)

Fresh lemon juice

Coarse kosher salt and freshly ground pepper

Whole-grain or sourdough bread, 1 slice

Small shallot, 1, minced

Lemon zest, 1 tablespoon grated

Fresh thyme, 1 tablespoon minced

makes 4 servings

● Preheat the oven to 450°F (230°C). Brush a rimmed baking sheet with olive oil. Place the fish, skin side down, on the pan; brush with olive oil and drizzle lightly with fresh lemon juice. Season lightly with salt and pepper and let marinate while preparing the topping.

● Tear the bread into 1-inch (2.5-cm) pieces. Place in a food processor and grind to fine crumbs. In a small bowl, combine ¾ cup (1½ oz/45 g) of the bread crumbs, the shallot, lemon zest, thyme, and 2 teaspoons olive oil. Mix to combine evenly. Season to taste with salt and pepper.

● Just before baking, divide the bread crumb mixture among the fillets, pressing onto the top of each piece. Bake until the fish is just springy to the touch and the bread crumbs start to brown, about 10 minutes.

● Transfer the fish to plates and serve right away.

quick tips

Arctic char or tilapia make great substitutes for the black cod. A nonstick olive oil spray is a great convenience item to keep on hand for quick meals. Use it here or in similar recipes to oil the baking pan.

Newly picked sugar snap peas, young green onions, and just a small amount of pork are the basis for a novel dish made with Japanese buckwheat noodles and bold Asian flavors. Finish the meal with ginger cookies and fresh strawberries.

stir-fried pork and sugar snaps with soba noodles

Low-sodium soy sauce,
3½ tablespoons

Cornstarch, 1½ teaspoons

Asian sesame oil,
1½ teaspoons, plus
1 tablespoon

Boneless center-cut pork chops or pork sirloin,
½ lb (250 g), cut across the grain into thin strips

Freshly ground black pepper

Rice wine vinegar,
2 tablespoons

Sugar, 1½ teaspoons

Sugar snap peas, ½ lb (250 g), strings removed and cut in half on the diagonal

Soba noodles, 6 oz (185 g)

Green onions, 1 bunch, white and green parts thinly sliced

Peanut oil, 1 tablespoon

Fresh ginger, 1 tablespoon peeled and minced

Red pepper flakes,
¼ teaspoon

makes 2 servings

In a bowl, combine 1½ tablespoons of the soy sauce and the cornstarch and stir to dissolve the cornstarch. Mix in 1½ teaspoons of the sesame oil. Add the pork and a generous amount of pepper and stir to coat. Let marinate for 15–30 minutes.

Meanwhile, in a small bowl combine the remaining 2 tablespoons soy sauce, remaining 1 tablespoon sesame oil, the vinegar, and sugar and stir to dissolve the sugar. Set aside.

Bring a large pot three-fourths full of water to a boil. Add the sugar snap peas and cook until just tender-crisp, about 4 minutes. Using a slotted spoon, transfer the peas to a bowl. Add the noodles to the boiling water and cook until just tender, stirring occasionally, about 4 minutes. Drain the noodles, and then return to the pot. Add ½ of the sauce to the noodles and stir to coat. Mix in the sugar snaps and all but 2 tablespoons of the green onions. Cover to keep warm.

In a large nonstick frying pan over medium-high heat, warm the peanut oil. Add the ginger and pepper flakes and stir until fragrant, about 5 seconds. Add the pork and separate the pieces. Stir constantly just until the pork is cooked through, 2–3 minutes. Add the remaining sauce and stir until the sauce thickens, about 30 seconds. Immediately add the pork and sauce to the noodles, and then toss to coat. Divide the noodles between 2 warmed plates. Sprinkle with the remaining green onions and serve right away.

quick tips

The recipe is also delicious at room temperature, so leftovers can be chilled overnight; bring them to room temperature before serving again. Double the quantity of ingredients to serve four.

Tarragon and baby broccoli are abundant in the spring. Here, the ingredients enhance quick-cooking turkey cutlets, which are an economical and healthful base for a meal. Hot cooked rice makes a smart, neutral side dish.

citrus-herb **turkey cutlets** with baby broccoli

Large orange, 1

Turkey breast cutlets,
1–1¼ lb (500–625 g)

Fresh tarragon, 1 tablespoon,
plus 1 teaspoon minced

**Coarse kosher salt and
freshly ground pepper**

Olive oil, 3 tablespoons

All-purpose flour
for dredging

Large shallot, 1, minced

Baby broccoli spears,
¾ lb (375 g)

Low-sodium chicken broth,
1 cup (8 fl oz/250 ml)

Unsalted butter,
½ tablespoon (optional)

makes 4 servings

● Finely grate the zest from the orange. Squeeze the juice from the orange and measure ¼ cup (2 fl oz/60 ml) juice. Sprinkle the turkey cutlets on both sides with the orange zest, 1 tablespoon of the tarragon, and salt and pepper.

● In a large nonstick frying pan over medium-high heat, warm 1 tablespoon of the oil. Dredge ½ of the turkey in the flour and shake off any excess; add to the frying pan and sauté until cooked through and golden brown, 2–3 minutes per side. Transfer the turkey to a warmed platter and tent with foil to keep warm. Add another tablespoon of the oil to the frying pan, and repeat dredging and cooking the remaining turkey.

● In the same pan over medium-high heat, warm the remaining 1 tablespoon of the oil. Add the shallot and sauté until beginning to brown, about 1 minute. Add the baby broccoli and the chicken broth. Cover and boil until the broccoli is just tender-crisp, about 5 minutes. Sprinkle the broccoli with salt and pepper, and using tongs, transfer the broccoli to the platter, arranging next to the turkey.

● Add the ¼ cup (2 fl oz/60 ml) orange juice to the frying pan and boil the liquid until it is reduced and almost syrupy, stirring frequently, about 3 minutes. Mix in the remaining 1 teaspoon tarragon. Swirl in the butter, if using. Taste and adjust the seasoning.

● Divide the turkey and broccoli among 4 warmed plates, pour the sauce over the turkey, and serve right away.

quick tips

For a quick salad for lunch or a light dinner the next day, cut the leftover turkey and broccoli into bite-size pieces, mix them into the remaining rice, and season with a bold vinaigrette.

Sugar snap peas and asparagus are at the peak of their season in spring and add crisp contrast to tender chicken. Sautéing the ingredients quickly in a small amount of oil keeps everything tasting clean. Serve over brown aromatic rice.

chicken sauté with sugar snaps and asparagus

All-purpose flour
for dredging

Chicken tenders, 10 oz (315 g)

Coarse kosher salt and freshly ground pepper

Olive oil, 2 tablespoons

Thin asparagus, 1 bunch (about ½ lb/250 g), ends trimmed

Sugar snap peas, ½ lb (250 g), strings removed

Low-sodium chicken broth, 1 cup (8 fl oz/250 ml)

Fresh thyme, 1 tablespoon minced, plus more for garnish

Fresh chives, 1 tablespoon minced, plus more for garnish

Fresh lemon juice, 2 tablespoons

Lemon zest strips for garnish (optional)

makes 2 servings; can be doubled

● Spread the flour on a plate. Cut the chicken tenders in half crosswise. Sprinkle with salt and pepper, then dredge in flour.

● In a large nonstick frying pan over medium-high heat, warm 1 tablespoon of the oil. Add the chicken and sauté until just cooked through, about 5 minutes. Transfer to a plate. Add the remaining 1 tablespoon oil to the frying pan, and reduce the heat to medium. Add the asparagus and sauté for 1 minute. Add the sugar snap peas; raise the heat to medium-high. Season the vegetables with salt and pepper and sauté for 1 minute. Add the broth and bring to a boil, stirring up the browned bits on the pan bottom. Cover the pan and boil until the vegetables are almost tender-crisp, about 3 minutes.

● Return the chicken to the pan. Add 1 tablespoon each thyme and chives and the lemon juice. Simmer uncovered until the sauce thickens and coats the chicken, stirring almost constantly, about 2 minutes. Taste and adjust the seasoning.

● Divide the chicken and vegetables between 2 warmed plates, garnish with thyme, chives, and lemon zest (if using) and serve right away.

quick tips

This recipe is a basic format for a quick sauté, and lends itself to endless variations, so you can use what's on hand in your refrigerator. Tarragon or basil would make tasty substitutes for the thyme (if using tarragon, use a little less). Fresh peas are a good alternative to the sugar snap peas and zucchini can replace the asparagus.

Tender, sweet Manila clams take only minutes to cook. Here, they're augmented by fresh fennel, saffron, and red pepper flakes for a sophisticated dish. Serve with crusty bread brushed with olive oil and sprinkled with black pepper.

clams with white beans, fennel, and broccoli rabe

Fennel bulb, 1, a few fronds reserved and minced for garnish

Fennel seeds, ½ teaspoon

Olive oil, 1 tablespoon, plus more as needed

Large red onion, ½, finely chopped

Red pepper flakes, ¼–½ teaspoon

Dry white wine, ½ cup (4 fl oz/125 ml)

Cannellini beans, 1 can (14½ oz/455 g), drained, juices reserved

Clam juice, 1 bottle (8 fl oz/250 ml)

Saffron threads

Freshly ground black pepper

Broccoli rabe or Chinese broccoli, ½ small bunch, chopped

Manila clams, 2 lb (1 kg), rinsed

Coarse kosher salt (optional)

makes 2 servings

● Cut the fennel bulb lengthwise into quarters, and then slice the quarters crosswise. In a mortar or spice mill, coarsely grind the fennel seeds.

● In a large nonstick frying pan over medium-high heat, warm 1 tablespoon of oil. Add the fennel bulb, fennel seeds, onion, and red pepper flakes. Sauté until the fennel and onion start to soften, about 5 minutes. Add the wine and boil until it evaporates, about 1 minute. Add the drained beans, clam juice, a large pinch of saffron, and a generous amount of black pepper, and simmer to blend the flavors, about 5 minutes. Add the broccoli rabe to the pan and simmer until it begins to wilt, about 1 minute. Add the clams. Stir in the reserved juice from the beans if the mixture is dry. Cover and boil until the clams open, about 5 minutes. Taste and adjust the seasoning, adding salt if needed.

● Divide the mixture between 2 warmed deep bowls. Drizzle with olive oil, sprinkle with fennel fronds, and serve right away.

quick tips

The recipe can be easily doubled, but use a large Dutch oven instead of a frying pan to accommodate the large quantity of clams. They need a little expanding room in order to steam properly.

As the weather starts to warm, summer marks the season for grilling. It is one of my favorite techniques for quickly cooked meals.

fresh & fast meals for **summer**

The abundant colors and textures of summer produce bring new dimension to my cooking. Every year, I wait eagerly for the truly ripe, deep-hued tomatoes; succulent eggplant and summer squash; and tender sweet corn that will enliven my seasonal suppers. Summer also marks the season for al fresco dining and grilling outdoors; often, I find I just can't face cooking over a hot stove. In this chapter, you'll discover nearly a month's worth of ideas for grilled, simmered, and quickly sautéed meals, all perfectly suited for the season.

summer market inspirations

- bell peppers
- chiles
- corn
- cucumbers
- eggplant
- green beans
- lettuce
- melons
- nectarines
- peaches
- plums
- summer squash
- tomatoes
- yellow crookneck squash
- zucchini

add a simple side

- Toss romaine lettuce, chopped cucumbers, tomatoes, and kalamata olives in a yogurt-and-herb–based dressing

- Using a vegetable peeler, cut zucchini into thin strips; boil in salted water until just tender and toss with olive oil and grated lemon zest

- Brush ears of corn with olive oil, sprinkle with salt and pepper, and grill over a hot fire, turning often, until tender-crisp, about 10 minutes

- Brush thick slices of country bread with olive oil, sprinkle with freshly ground pepper, and grill over a hot fire, turning once, until lightly marked by the grill, about 2 minutes per side

choose fruit for dessert

- Brush pitted and halved yellow peaches with melted butter and grill over a medium-hot fire until well browned, about 8 minutes; sprinkle with crumbled amaretti cookies or gingersnaps

- Cut plums into thin slices and serve with mango, raspberry, or other fruit sorbet

- Cut ripe cantaloupe, honeydew, or watermelon into wedges, chill thoroughly, and serve with sea salt and chile powder for sprinkling

smart strategies for summer meals

stock the summer pantry For the warm months to come, add a few bold spices and condiments to your collection to bring punch to summer meals. I like cayenne pepper, ground coriander, ground cinnamon, smoked paprika, and canned chipotle chiles in adobo sauce.

storing fresh herbs If you don't have a cutting garden, you can stand purchased bunches of parsley, basil, or cilantro in a glass of water and keep it on the kitchen counter to snip fresh herbs as needed. The herbs will stay fresh for several days. Wrap other herbs in a damp paper towel, slip them into a plastic bag, and store in the refrigerator crisper.

tips for grilling When setting up the grill for cooking, It is useful to leave a section of it free of coals. This creates a cooler area to where you can move food to help manage flare-ups. If you have a gas grill, be sure to preheat it with the cover closed for 10–15 minutes before grilling.

grilling indoors If you don't own an outdoor grill, or in the event of inclement weather, you can typically use a broiler using the same timing as for grilling. Or, try a stove-top grill pan, ideally made from cast iron. In either case, be sure to turn on your kitchen ventilation to control odors.

consider the weather When hot temperatures are in the forecast, choose dishes that you don't need to cook, such as a big salad supplemented by a purchased rotisserie chicken. Hot summer evenings are also welcome occasions for serving leftovers from a previous night's meal.

summer

Iconic summer ingredients, eggplant, cherry tomatoes, and fresh basil, make a tempting pizza topping. Cooking the vegetables—and the pizza—on the grill keeps the kitchen cool and adds a hint of smokiness. Serve with a green salad.

grilled pizza with eggplant and tomatoes

Extra-virgin olive oil, ¼ cup (2 fl oz/60 ml), plus more as needed

Balsamic vinegar, ¼ cup (2 fl oz/60 ml)

Coarse kosher salt and freshly ground black pepper

Asian eggplants, 2 (about ½ lb/250 g total weight), cut lengthwise into ⅓-inch (9-mm) slices

Small red onion, 1, cut crosswise into ⅓-inch (9-mm) slices

Pizza dough (see tips), 1 lb (500 g)

Fresh whole-milk mozzarella cheese, ½ lb (250 g), shredded

Small cherry tomatoes, 1 cup (6 oz/185 g) halved crosswise

Romano cheese, ½ cup (2 oz/60 g) grated

Red pepper flakes, ½ teaspoon

Fresh basil, 3 tablespoons slivered

Fresh marjoram, 2 tablespoons minced

makes 2 pizzas; 4 servings

● Prepare a charcoal or gas grill for direct-heat cooking over medium heat. In a bowl, whisk together the ¼ cup (2 fl oz/60 ml) oil and the vinegar; season with salt and black pepper. Arrange the eggplant and onion slices on a rimmed baking sheet. Brush lightly with the vinegar-oil mixture. Place the eggplant and onion on the grill, cover, and cook until tender and browned, about 5 minutes per side for the eggplant and 6 minutes per side for the onion. Remove from the grill. Cut the eggplant into 1½-inch (4-cm) pieces. Separate the onion slices into rings.

● Divide the pizza dough in half. On a lightly floured surface, roll out each half to a 9-inch (23-cm) round. Transfer to a floured baking sheet. Brush the top of each round with olive oil and sprinkle with black pepper. Place the crusts, oiled side down, on the grill, cover, and grill until bottoms are firm and browned, about 3 minutes. Turn the crusts over, cover, and grill until the bottoms are just set, about 2 minutes. Transfer the crusts to the baking sheet, grill-marked side up.

● Spread ½ of the mozzarella over each dough round, and then top with the eggplant, onion, and tomatoes. Sprinkle ½ of the romano cheese and ½ of the pepper flakes over each. Whisk the vinegar-oil mixture and drizzle about 2 teaspoons over each pizza. Using a large spatula, transfer the pizzas to the grill. Cover and grill until the cheeses melt, 5–8 minutes.

● Transfer the pizzas to a cutting board. Sprinkle with the herbs. Cut into wedges, place on 2 warmed platters, and serve right away.

quick tips

Use purchased fresh pizza dough (not dough from a tube) for quick weeknight cooking, or follow the recipe on page 232. Pizzas are easy to vary. A few of my favorite ways include replacing the pecorino with Parmesan; using fontina instead of mozzarella; or using zucchini instead of eggplant.

Frittatas and other egg dishes are underappreciated dinner entrées. Here, a charred poblano chile adds a smoky flavor to contrast to the richness of the other ingredients. Accompany with a tossed green salad and grilled bread.

zucchini, chile, and red onion **frittata**

Poblano chile, 1

Large eggs, 8

Coarse kosher salt and freshly ground pepper

White Cheddar cheese, ¼ lb (125 g), coarsely shredded

Olive oil, 1 tablespoon

Red onion, 1, halved, then sliced

Zucchini, 2, cut into quarters lengthwise, then sliced crosswise

Fresh cilantro, chopped

makes 4 servings

● Using tongs or a long fork, hold the chile over the flame of a gas burner, turning it until the skin is evenly blistered and blackened. (Alternatively, place the chile on a baking sheet and broil, turning as needed and watching carefully to prevent burning.) Transfer the chile to a bag and let cool. Rub the charred peel off the chile. Cut the chile in half, remove the seeds, and finely chop.

● In a bowl, combine the eggs, ½ teaspoon salt, and ½ teaspoon pepper. Beat with a fork to blend. Mix in ¾ cup (3 oz/90 g) of the cheese.

● In a 10-inch (25-cm) ovenproof frying pan, ideally nonstick, over medium-high heat, warm the olive oil. Add the onion and sauté until almost tender, about 6 minutes. Add the zucchini, sprinkle with salt and pepper, and sauté until tender, about 5 minutes. Mix in the chile. Pour the egg mixture into the frying pan, and gently stir to distribute evenly. Reduce the heat to medium-low, cover, and cook until the eggs are almost set but still moist in the center, about 10 minutes.

● Meanwhile, preheat the broiler. Sprinkle the remaining cheese over the frittata. Broil until the eggs puff, the center is springy to the touch, and the cheese begins to brown, about 3 minutes. Using a flexible spatula, loosen the frittata around the edges. Slide the frittata onto a platter, and sprinkle cilantro over the top. Serve warm or at room temperature, cutting into wedges.

quick tips

This frittata takes only a few minutes to prepare, but for even quicker cooking, chop the chile and sauté it with the onion rather than charring it. You can also replace the chile with a red, orange, or yellow bell pepper. Serve leftovers at room temperature as an appetizer.

68

This thick sauce shows off summer basil at its best and is the perfect accent for the gentle flavor of albacore tuna. Grill olive oil–rubbed bread along with the fish, and serve briefly sautéed zucchini ribbons on the side.

grilled tuna with basil-walnut sauce

Albacore tuna steaks,
2 (about 6 oz/185 g each),
1 inch (2.5 cm) thick

Coarse kosher salt and freshly ground pepper

Grated zest of 1 lemon

Extra-virgin olive oil,
1½ tablespoons, plus
more as needed

Fresh basil leaves, ¼ cup
(¼ oz/7 g) packed

Walnut pieces, 1 tablespoon

makes 2 servings;
can be doubled

● Place the tuna on a plate. Sprinkle both sides with salt, pepper, and the lemon zest. Brush with olive oil. Let marinate while preparing the sauce.

● In the work bowl of a food processor, combine the basil, walnuts, ⅛ teaspoon salt, and a generous amount of pepper. Process until finely ground. With the machine running, gradually add 1½ tablespoons olive oil. Taste the sauce and adjust the seasoning with salt and pepper.

● Prepare a charcoal or gas grill for direct-heat grilling over high heat. Add the tuna, cover the grill, and cook as desired, about 3 minutes per side for rare. Transfer the tuna to 2 warmed individual plates. Top each with the basil sauce and serve right away.

quick tips

The sauce takes just a moment to prepare—simply purée the herb leaves, oil, and, nuts in a food processor. If the sauce seems too thick, you can thin it with additional oil. It is also great on any fish or chicken, or mixed into potato salad, and is easy to double.

Fresh summer vegetables and cheese enrobed in an easy buttermilk-cornmeal batter make a terrific meatless main course. Serve with a salad of romaine hearts tossed with chickpeas and a lemon-yogurt dressing.

corn and cheddar fritters with sautéed tomatoes

Olive oil, 2 tablespoons, plus more as needed

Red onion, ½, finely chopped

Red bell pepper, ½, finely chopped

Corn kernels, cut from 1 large ear

Coarse kosher salt and freshly ground pepper

Cornmeal, ⅔ cup (3.5 oz/105 g)

All-purpose flour, 3 tablespoons

Sugar, 1 teaspoon

Cayenne pepper, ¼ teaspoon, plus ⅛ teaspoon

Baking soda, ⅛ teaspoon

Buttermilk, ½ cup (4 fl oz/125 ml)

Large egg, 1

Sharp Cheddar cheese, 1 cup (3.5 oz/105 g) finely diced or shredded

Fresh basil, 2 tablespoons minced, plus small leaves for garnish

Grape or cherry tomatoes, 10–12 oz (315–375 g), halved

Makes about 8 fritters, or 2 servings

● In a large frying pan over medium-high heat, warm 1 tablespoon of the oil. Add ½ of the onion and all of the bell pepper and sauté until they begin to soften, about 3 minutes. Add the corn and season with salt and pepper. Sauté until the corn begins to soften, about 2 minutes. Transfer to a bowl to cool.

● In a medium bowl, combine the cornmeal, flour, sugar, ⅛ teaspoon of the cayenne, baking soda, and ¼ teaspoon salt; stir to blend. In a small bowl, combine the buttermilk and egg; beat with a fork to blend. Add the wet ingredients to the dry ingredients, and stir until just combined. Fold in the sautéed vegetables, cheese, and the 2 tablespoons basil.

● In a clean frying pan over medium heat, warm 1 tablespoon oil. Add the remaining ½ cup onion and sauté until it begins to soften, about 2 minutes. Add the tomatoes, season with salt and pepper, and sauté until starting to soften, about 2 minutes. Transfer to a small bowl. Stir in the remaining ¼ teaspoon cayenne, and then cover to keep warm.

● In a clean large frying pan over medium heat, warm a thin film of olive oil. Working in batches and adding more oil as needed, use a ¼-cup (2–fl oz/60-ml) measure to add the batter to the pan. Cook until golden, about 2 minutes on each side. Transfer to a warmed platter, and cover to keep warm. Divide the fritters between 2 warmed plates. Spoon the tomato mixture over the fritters, garnish with small basil leaves, and serve right away.

quick tips

These fritters can be prepared and cooked 1 day in advance and refrigerated. Reheat them in a 350°F (180°C) oven until crisp and heated through, about 6 minutes. If you don't have buttermilk on hand, mix 1 teaspoon white vinegar into whole, low-fat, or soy milk and let stand for 5 minutes.

This big salad, made with cooked chicken, is perfect for a hot night when you don't want to cook. Bold chipotle chiles perk up the lemon-basil dressing. Serve it with crusty bread and finish with cooling slices of fresh melon.

chopped salad with lemon-chipotle dressing

Roast chicken, 1 (2 lb/1 kg)

Dijon mustard,
2 tablespoons

Fresh lemon juice,
2 tablespoons

Olive oil, 6 tablespoons
(3 fl oz/90 ml)

Fresh basil, ⅓ cup
(⅓ oz/10 g) minced

Shallot, 1, minced

**Canned chipotle
chiles in adobo sauce,**
1–1½ teaspoons minced
with sauce

**Coarse kosher salt and
freshly ground pepper**

Persian or Asian cucumbers,
2, halved lengthwise, cut
crosswise into ½-inch
(12-mm) pieces

Heirloom tomatoes, 2, diced

Red bell pepper, 1, diced

Romaine hearts, 1–2,
trimmed and chopped

Large avocado, 1, firm but
ripe, diced

makes 4 servings

● Pull the chicken meat from the bones, discarding the skin. Cut the meat into bite-size pieces and transfer to a large salad bowl. In a small bowl, combine the mustard and lemon juice and whisk to blend. Gradually whisk in the olive oil. Mix in the basil, shallot, and chipotle with its sauce. Season the dressing to taste with salt and pepper. Mix ¼ cup (2 fl oz/60 ml) dressing into the chicken and let marinate while preparing the remaining ingredients.

● Mix the cucumbers, tomatoes, and bell pepper into the chicken. Mix in the lettuce. Add enough dressing to lightly coat the ingredients. Taste and adjust the seasoning. Gently mix in the avocado and serve.

quick tips

Purchase a rotisserie chicken from your local market—it takes only minutes to pull the meat from the bones and cut it into bite-size pieces. The dressing can be made 1 day ahead and refrigerated; mix in the vegetables just before serving. For a meatless version, replace the chicken pieces with 2 cans (15 oz/ 470 g each) chickpeas. Simmer the beans with ½ cup (4 fl oz/125 ml) water and ¼ cup (2 fl oz/60 ml) of the dressing for 5 minutes; cool before using.

Assorted peppers, quickly sautéed, make a garden-fresh base for grilled steak. A soy-based marinade elevates the flavor of the steak in the time it takes to cut the vegetables. Grill slices of rustic bread with the meat for a complete dinner.

grilled steak with sweet peppers

summer

Low-sodium soy sauce,
¼ cup (2 fl oz/60 ml)

Olive oil, ¼ cup (2 fl oz/
60 ml) plus 1 tablespoon

Honey, 2 tablespoons

Large shallots, 2, minced

Fresh rosemary,
2½ tablespoons minced

**Coarse kosher salt and
freshly ground black pepper**

**Flank steak or
top sirloin steak,**
1¼ lb (625 g) about
1 inch (2.5 cm) thick

Large red bell pepper,
1, thinly sliced

Large yellow bell pepper,
1, thinly sliced

Large poblano chile,
1, thinly sliced

Large red onion,
1, thinly sliced

Red pepper flakes,
½ teaspoon

**Sherry vinegar or
balsamic vinegar,**
2 tablespoons

makes 4 servings

• In a shallow glass baking pan, combine the soy sauce, ¼ cup (2 fl oz/60 ml) of the oil, honey, shallots, 1½ tablespoons rosemary, ½ teaspoon salt, and black pepper. Mix to combine. Pat the steak dry. Add the steak to the pan, and turn to coat with the marinade. Let marinate while preparing the peppers.

• Prepare a charcoal or gas grill for direct-heat cooking over high heat.

• In a large nonstick frying pan over medium-high heat, warm the remaining 1 tablespoon oil. Add the bell peppers, poblano chile, and onion. Season with salt and pepper and sauté until tender, about 8 minutes. Mix in the remaining 1 tablespoon rosemary and the pepper flakes, and cook, stirring, for 30 seconds. Add the vinegar and stir until absorbed. Remove the pan from the heat.

• Remove the meat from the marinade. Add the steak to the grill and cook as desired, about 4 minutes per side for medium-rare. Transfer the meat to a work surface and let rest 5 minutes.

• Warm the pepper mixture and divide among 4 plates. Slice the steak thinly on an angle. Arrange the steak on top of the peppers and serve right away.

quick tips

Flank steak or top sirloin are flavorful cuts for weeknight cooking, but sometimes I splurge on a tender rib-eye or New York strip for this recipe. The peppers can be cooked 1 day ahead of time and refrigerated. Bring them to room temperature or warm in a frying pan over medium heat before serving. Leftovers make great steak sandwiches, or can be served as a salad the next night with a simple vinaigrette made with sherry vinegar.

I season these satisfying vegetarian tacos with fennel seeds, which lend the anise-like flavor of the avocado leaves used to flavor beans in Mexico. If you like, make a double batch of the salsa and serve it with chips to start off the meal.

black bean tacos with avocado salsa

White onion, 1, finely chopped

Large plum tomatoes, 2, halved, seeded, and finely diced

Serrano chile, 1, seeded and minced

Fresh cilantro, ¼ cup (⅓ oz/10 g) minced

Fresh lime juice, 3 tablespoons, plus lime wedges for garnish

Avocado, 1, pitted, peeled, and finely diced

Coarse kosher salt and freshly ground pepper

Olive oil, 2 tablespoons

Large red bell pepper, 1, diced

Fresh corn kernels, cut from 1 ear of corn

Corn tortillas, 6 inches (15 cm) in diameter, 8–12

Fennel seeds or anise seeds, ¼ teaspoon

Black beans, 2 cans (15 oz/470 g each), drained, liquid reserved

Feta cheese, crumbled

makes 4 servings

● In a bowl, combine ¼ cup (1 oz/30 g) of the onion, the tomatoes, chile, cilantro, and lime juice. Gently mix in the avocado. Season the mixture to taste with salt and pepper.

● In a large nonstick frying pan over medium-high heat, warm 1 tablespoon of the oil. Add the bell pepper, season with salt and pepper, and sauté until it starts to soften, about 7 minutes. Add the corn kernels, reduce the heat to medium, and sauté until it begins to soften, about 2 minutes. Adjust the seasoning with salt and pepper. Transfer the mixture to a bowl and cover to keep warm.

● Toast the tortillas over a gas flame or on a griddle just until they give off the fragrance of toasted corn, about 20 seconds on each side; then, wrap the tortillas in foil to keep warm.

● In the same frying pan over medium heat, warm the remaining 1 tablespoon oil. Add the remaining onion and the fennel seeds, and sauté until the onion is almost tender, about 5 minutes. Add the beans by very large spoonfuls, mashing and stirring each addition before adding the next. Thin the bean mixture to a coarse, thick purée with the reserved liquid. Season to taste with salt and pepper.

● Place the salsa, bell pepper mixture, bean mixture, feta, tortillas, and lime wedges on the table, allowing diners to assemble their own tacos.

quick tips

The sautéed vegetables and black beans can be made 1 day ahead and stored in the refrigerator. Warm the beans over medium heat, thinning them with water as needed, and stir the vegetables in a frying pan over medium heat to warm through. The black beans also are great with chips, so make extra, and serve as a starter another night.

Pomegranate molasses and fresh mint lend exotic flavors to the lamb. Colorful vegetable skewers cook alongside. Serve with quick-cooking couscous; for extra flavor, cook it in chicken broth with sautéed onions, turmeric, and cumin.

lamb kebabs with pomegranate glaze

Pomegranate molasses, ¼ cup (2 fl oz/60 ml)

Shallot, 1, minced

Olive oil, 3 tablespoons

Cumin seeds, 2 teaspoons crushed in a mortar with a pestle

Boneless leg of lamb, 1¼ lb (625 g), well trimmed and cut into 1-inch (2.5-cm) cubes

Zucchini, 2, halved lengthwise, cut into 1-inch (2.5-cm) pieces

Large red bell pepper, 1, cut into 1-inch (2.5-cm) squares

Red onion, 1, cut into 1-inch (2.5-cm) squares

Coarse kosher salt and freshly ground pepper

Fresh mint leaves, slivered

makes 4 servings

● Soak 12 bamboo skewers in water to cover for 30 minutes.

● Meanwhile, in a medium bowl, combine the pomegranate molasses, shallot, 1 tablespoon of the olive oil, and 1 teaspoon of the cumin seeds; mix well. Add the lamb and stir to coat. In a large bowl, combine the zucchini, bell pepper, onion, remaining 2 tablespoons oil, and remaining 1 teaspoon cumin seeds. Sprinkle with salt and pepper and stir to coat.

● Prepare a charcoal or gas grill for direct-heat grilling over high heat. Drain the skewers. Divide the lamb among 4 skewers; reserve the glaze remaining in the bowl. Sprinkle the lamb with salt and pepper. Divide the vegetables among 8 skewers, arranging them as you like. Brush the vegetables with the remaining glaze. Place the skewers on the grill. Cover the grill and cook the lamb as desired and the vegetables until they begin to brown and soften, about 5 minutes per side for medium-rare lamb and 6 minutes per side for the vegetables.

● Sprinkle the skewers with mint and serve right away.

quick tips

If you prefer an alternative to red meat, replace the lamb with skinless boneless chicken thighs. Pomegranate molasses is a thick syrup made from pomegranate juice. It can be found at many supermarkets, in Middle Eastern stores, or ordered from mail-order sources. The marinade can be made 1 day ahead of time; store in the refrigerator.

Here, I've transformed familiar chicken breasts and fresh corn with vibrant smoked paprika and fresh lime juice. Cooking them on the grill heightens the smoky flavor. Serve with a green salad and finish with sliced peaches.

grilled chicken and corn with smoked paprika rub

Smoked paprika,
1 tablespoon

Ground cumin, 1 tablespoon

Olive oil, 3 tablespoons

Fresh lime juice,
3 tablespoons

Chicken breast cutlets,
1¼–1½ lb (625–750 g)

Corn, 4 ears, husked

Coarse kosher salt and freshly ground pepper

Grated lime zest,
1½ tablespoons

Fresh thyme, 1½ tablespoons minced

makes 4 servings

• In a small bowl, combine the paprika and cumin. Gradually mix in the olive oil and lime juice. Place the chicken and corn on a large baking sheet. Brush on all sides with the paprika mixture, and then sprinkle with salt and pepper.

• Prepare a charcoal or gas grill for direct-heat grilling over high heat. Add the corn to the grill rack, cover, and cook until it starts to brown in spots and almost tender, turning frequently, about 10 minutes. Add the chicken to the grill rack, cover, and cook until the chicken is springy to the touch and cooked through, about 2½ minutes per side. Transfer the chicken and corn to a warmed platter. Sprinkle with lime zest and thyme, and serve right away.

quick tips

In the event of inclement weather, the chicken is equally good sautéed. In that case, boil the corn, and season it after cooking. Leftover chicken makes great sandwiches, or you can cut up the chicken, cut the kernels from the corn ears, and add them both to a salad.

A combination of lemon and lime zest adds tang to simply roasted fish fillets. A vinaigrette using the juice from the lemon makes a sprightly sauce to pour over the cooked fish. Serve with boiled red potatoes and sautéed zucchini.

roasted mahi mahi with citrus vinaigrette

Lemon, 1

Olive oil for brushing

Mahi mahi fillets, 4 (about 5–6 oz/155–185 g each)

Lemon zest, 4 teaspoons grated

Lime zest, 4 teaspoons grated

Coarse kosher salt and freshly ground pepper

Dijon mustard, 2 teaspoons

Extra-virgin olive oil, ⅓ cup (3 fl oz/80 ml)

Shallot, 1, minced

makes 4 servings

● Cut the whole lemon in half. Set aside 1 lemon half, then squeeze 2 tablespoons juice from the other ½ lemon.

● Preheat the oven to 400°F (200°C). Brush a small rimmed baking sheet with olive oil, then place the fish fillets on the sheet. Brush the fish fillets all over with olive oil, rub in the lemon and lime zests, and then squeeze the juice from the ½ lemon over the fish. Sprinkle with salt and pepper. Roast until the fillets are just opaque in the center, about 10 minutes.

● Meanwhile, in a small glass measuring cup or small bowl, place the mustard. Whisk in the 2 tablespoons lemon juice. Gradually whisk in the extra-virgin olive oil. Mix in the shallot. Season the vinaigrette to taste with salt and pepper.

● Transfer the fish to warmed plates, spoon a little of the vinaigrette over the top, and serve right away.

quick tips

It's easiest to zest citrus fruits when they are whole, so in recipes calling for both, remove the zest from the fruit before cutting it in half for juicing. This dessing can be prepared 1 day in advance and refrigerated; bring it to room temperature before serving. It would also be good on tuna or halibut. You can also make extra dressing and use it to dress a salad on another night.

This meatless pasta dish shows that if you start with fresh ingredients, it takes very little work to make a stellar meal. Olives and feta cheese add richness and walnuts add crunch to this dish, but you can omit any of these if you wish.

pasta with grilled vegetables and herbs

Zucchini, 2, cut lengthwise in thirds

Red bell pepper, 1, cut into quarters

Yellow bell pepper, 1, cut into quarters

Large red onion, 1, cut crosswise into slices ½–¾ inch (12 mm–2 cm) thick

Olive oil for brushing

Coarse kosher salt and freshly ground pepper

Penne, ½ lb (250 g), preferably multigrain

Extra-virgin olive oil, 3 tablespoons

Mixed fresh herbs, such as mint, basil, oregano, and marjoram, ½ cup (¾ oz/20 g) minced

Small red chile, 1, minced

Pitted kalamata olives, ¼ cup (1½ oz/45 g) finely chopped

Walnuts, ¼ cup (1 oz/30 g) finely chopped

Feta cheese, ½ cup (2½ oz/ 75 g) finely chopped, or a small chunk of romano cheese

makes 4 servings

● Prepare a charcoal or gas grill for direct-heat cooking over high heat. Arrange the vegetables in a single layer on a large rimmed baking sheet. Brush with olive oil and sprinkle with salt and pepper on both sides. Arrange the vegetables on the grill, cover, and cook until tender and lightly browned, about 5 minutes per side. Remove from the grill and cut into 1-inch (2.5-cm) pieces.

● Meanwhile, bring a large pot three-fourths full of salted water to a boil. Add the pasta, stir well, and cook until al dente, about 11 minutes.

● Drain the pasta and transfer to a warmed shallow serving bowl. Add the grilled vegetables, extra-virgin olive oil, fresh herbs, chile, olives, and walnuts to the pasta and toss to combine. Season to taste with salt and pepper. If using feta cheese, sprinkle over and toss to combine. If using romano cheese, allow the diners to grate it over their own serving at the table.

quick tips

For vibrance, I use a combination of herbs—basil, mint, marjoram, and oregano. To simplify, one or two herbs could be used instead. Leftovers are satisfying another night; serve at room temperature, or stir them over medium heat, adding water as needed to prevent sticking. For ease, replace the fresh chile with a pinch of red pepper flakes.

This simple, lemony dressing shows off both the briny shrimp and sweet summer squash. For an easy side dish, brush slices of rustic bread with olive oil and grill them alongside the shrimp and squash until golden grill marks form.

grilled shrimp and summer squash

Dijon mustard, 2 teaspoons

Lemon zest, grated from 1 lemon

Fresh lemon juice, 2 tablespoons

Extra-virgin olive oil, ⅓ cup (3 fl oz/80 ml), plus more as needed

Small serrano chile, 1, seeded and minced

Fresh marjoram, 1 teaspoon minced

Fresh basil, 1 tablespoon minced

Coarse kosher salt and freshly ground pepper

Colossal shrimp, 1¼ lb (625 g), peeled and deveined with tails intact

Summer squash, 8, cut lengthwise into 3 pieces each

makes 4 servings

• Soak bamboo skewers in water to cover for 30 minutes. Prepare a charcoal or gas grill for direct-heat cooking over medium-high heat.

• Add the mustard to a small bowl. Add the lemon zest and juice and mix well. Gradually whisk in ⅓ cup (3 fl oz/80 ml) olive oil. Mix in the chile and herbs. Season the sauce to taste with salt and pepper.

• Drain the skewers. Thread about 4 of the shrimp on a skewer, and then thread a second skewer through the shrimp, parallel to the first, to prevent the shrimp from spinning around on the skewers. Repeat with the remaining shrimp. Place the squash slices and shrimp on a large baking sheet. Brush the shrimp and squash with olive oil, and sprinkle with salt and pepper.

• Arrange the squash on the grill, cover, and cook until tender and lightly charred, about 5 minutes per side. Transfer to a plate. Place the shrimp on the grill and cook, uncovered, until just cooked through, about 4 minutes per side. Remove the shrimp from the skewers and cut the squash crosswise.

• Transfer the shrimp and squash to a medium bowl and toss with the lemon-herb sauce. Season to taste with salt and pepper and serve right away.

quick tips

Vary the recipe by using red bell peppers in place of the summer squash, or scallops instead of shrimp. Chicken breasts would also be good with these seasonings. To save time, make the dressing 1 day ahead and refrigerate. Bring it to room temperature before using.

Briny mussels, sweet tomatoes, and pungent basil make a perfect accent for pasta. Round out the meal with a simple salad. Since the dish is so lean, you can indulge in dessert—try vanilla gelato with toasted coconut and anisette.

spaghetti and mussels with tomatoes and basil

Spaghetti, preferably multigrain, 6 oz (185 g)

Olive oil, 2 tablespoons

Large shallot, 1, minced

Red pepper flakes, ⅛–¼ teaspoon

Mussels, 1 lb (500 g)

Dry white wine, ⅓ cup (3 fl oz/80 ml)

Grated lemon zest, 1 teaspoon

Cherry tomatoes, ¾ lb (375 g), halved

Fresh basil, ½ cup slivered (¾ oz/20 g)

Extra-virgin olive oil, 1 tablespoon

Coarse kosher salt and freshly ground black pepper

makes 2 servings

● Bring a large pot three-fourths full of salted water to a boil. Add the pasta, stir well, and cook until al dente, about 11 minutes.

● Meanwhile, in a heavy large frying pan over medium-high heat, warm the oil. Add the shallot and pepper flakes and sauté until the shallot is almost tender, about 2 minutes. Add the mussels, wine, and lemon zest. Cover the pan and cook until the mussel shells begin to open, about 4 minutes. Add the tomatoes and cook until starting to soften, stirring frequently, about 2 minutes. Discard any mussels that do not open.

● Drain the pasta and transfer to a warmed large shallow bowl. Pour the mussels and sauce over the pasta. Add the basil and 1 tablespoon extra-virgin olive oil and toss to coat the pasta. Season to taste with salt and pepper, and serve right away.

quick tips

The sauce takes such little time to prepare, it can be made while the pasta cooks. The mussel mixture would be equally delicious served in shallow bowls accompanied by crusty bread, rather than over pasta, to soak up the juices. For an extra special touch, brush the bread with olive oil and then grill or broil until golden and crunchy on the edges.

What is great about this recipe is that the fresh summer corn and tomatoes double as both sauce and vegetable and cook in the same frying pan used to sear the turkey. Offer rice, quinoa, bulgur wheat, or couscous on the side.

turkey cutlets with fresh corn and tomatoes

Turkey breast cutlets,
1–1¼ lb (500–625 g)

Sweet paprika, 1¾ teaspoons

Ground cumin, 1 teaspoon

**Coarse kosher salt and
freshly ground pepper**

Olive oil, 2 tablespoons

Small red onion, ¼, finely
chopped

Red pepper flakes,
¼–½ teaspoon

Corn kernels, cut from
3 ears, about 2 cups
(¾ lb/375 g)

Grape or cherry tomatoes,
10–12 oz (315–375 g), halved

Low-sodium chicken broth,
½ cup (4 fl oz/60 ml)

Fresh marjoram,
2 tablespoons minced

makes 4 servings

Sprinkle the turkey with 1 teaspoon of the paprika and the cumin, and then season lightly with salt and pepper. In a large nonstick frying pan over medium heat, warm 1 tablespoon of the oil. Add the turkey, in batches if necessary, and sauté until browned and just cooked through, about 3 minutes per side. Transfer the cooked turkey to a warmed platter and tent with foil to keep warm.

In the same frying pan over medium heat, warm the remaining 1 tablespoon oil. Add the onion and pepper flakes and cook until the onion begins to soften, about 1 minute. Add the corn, and then sprinkle with salt and pepper. Sauté until the corn begins to soften, about 3 minutes. Add the tomatoes and cook until soft and juicy, about 2 minutes. Mix in the remaining ¾ teaspoon paprika and then the broth and any juices on the turkey platter. Boil until the liquid is syrupy, about 1 minute. Mix in the marjoram.

Taste and adjust the seasoning. Spoon the corn-tomato mixture over the turkey and serve right away.

quick tips

If you are cooking for two, eat half of this for one meal. Then, cut up the leftover turkey and mix it and the vegetables into the leftover rice or other grain, season with a vinaigrette, and save for another meal. Or, cut the turkey into bite-size pieces, re-heat with the vegetables in olive oil, and toss with pasta; stir in a little of the pasta cooking water to add moisture.

Here, baby back ribs are soaked in a soy-lime-chile mixture and then quickly grilled. An herb salad offers a refreshing counterpoint to the richness of the meat. Offer purchased sushi as a starter and end with chilled watermelon slices.

spicy asian-style **baby back ribs**

Fresh ginger, ⅓ cup (3 oz/90 g) peeled and minced

Shallots, 2, minced

Serrano chiles, 2, seeded and minced

Sugar, ¼ cup (2 oz/60 g)

Low-sodium soy sauce ¼ cup (2 fl oz/60 ml)

Fresh lime juice, ¼ cup (2 fl oz/60 ml)

Baby back pork ribs, 1¾–2 lb (875 g–1 kg), cut into 2-rib sections

Coarse kosher salt and freshly ground pepper

Herb salad mix, 3 cups (3 oz/90 g)

makes 2 servings; can be doubled

● In a small bowl, combine the ginger, shallots, chiles, sugar, soy sauce, and lime juice; mix to dissolve the sugar. Place the ribs on a rimmed baking sheet. Sprinkle generously on both sides with salt and pepper. Spoon 2 tablespoons of the ginger mixture over each side of the ribs, and rub in; let marinate while preparing the grill. Mix ¼ cup (2 fl oz/60 ml) water into the remaining ginger mixture and reserve to use as a sauce.

● Prepare a charcoal or gas grill for direct-heat grilling over medium heat. Place the ribs on the grill rack, meat side up, and cook for 8 minutes. Turn over and cook for another 8 minutes. Cover and grill the ribs until cooked through, about 8 minutes longer on each side.

● Transfer the ribs to a cutting board and cut apart into individual ribs. Divide the salad between 2 plates and then top with the ribs. Spoon some of the reserved ginger sauce over the top and serve right away.

quick tips

This recipe yields a generous amount of the piquant sauce, and leftovers can be served with shrimp, fish, or chicken. Although spare ribs generally need to bake for over an hour before grilling, baby back ribs are tender enough to be quickly grilled without precooking—perfect for weeknight meals.

Fresh dill, green onions, lemon, mustard, and fruity extra-virgin olive oil are the vivid seasonings of this main course salad. When steaming green beans, take care not to overcook them to retain their fresh green color.

shrimp salad with potatoes and green beans

summer

Lemon, 1 wedge, plus 2 tablespoons lemon juice

Green onions, 4, white and pale green parts finely chopped, trimmings reserved

Fresh dill, 3 tablespoons minced, stems reserved

Boiling potatoes, ¾ lb (375 g), cut into 1-inch (2.5-cm) pieces

Green beans, ¾ lb (375 g), cut into 1½-inch (4-cm) pieces

Whole-grain Dijon mustard, 1 teaspoon

Extra-virgin olive oil, 3 tablespoons

Coarse kosher salt and freshly ground pepper

Large shrimp, ¾ lb (375 g), peeled and deveined

makes 2 servings

• Fill a small saucepan three-fourths full with water. Add the lemon wedge, green onion trimmings, and dill stems. Bring to a boil. Cover, reduce the heat to low, and simmer to blend flavors while cooking the vegetables.

• In a steamer over boiling water, steam the potatoes until just tender, about 15 minutes. Transfer the potatoes to a colander, drain briefly, and then transfer to a large bowl. Using a rubber spatula, gently mix in 1 tablespoon of the lemon juice. Add the green beans to the steamer and steam until just tender-crisp, about 6 minutes. Transfer the beans to a colander, drain briefly, and then add to the potatoes. In a small bowl, combine the mustard and remaining 1 tablespoon lemon juice. Gradually whisk in the oil. Add to the potatoes and green beans. Add the green onions and dill, and mix gently to combine.

• Raise the heat to high and bring the simmering seasoned water to a boil. Add 1 tablespoon salt and the shrimp. Return the water to a boil. Reduce the heat and simmer until the shrimp are just cooked through, about 2 minutes. Drain well.

• Cut the shrimp into ¾-inch (2-cm) pieces and add to the salad. Toss to combine. Season the salad to taste with salt and pepper, and serve right away.

quick tips

This recipe doubles easily and can be made 1 day ahead of time. If you are cooking for two, consider doubling the recipe and serving it again for an extra-quick dinner the next night. For a sustainable product, look for wild American shrimp. For even faster preparation, use purchased cooked shrimp that has already been peeled.

When I want the smoky taste of grilling, but I'm not inclined to light the coals, smoked paprika is the perfect seasoning. Here, it accents sautéed steak pieces paired with fresh corn kernels and summer herbs in a meal-in-one pasta dish.

pasta with seared steak, corn, and zucchini

Top sirloin or rib eye steak,
1–1¼ lb (500–625 g)

Smoked hot paprika,
2¼ teaspoons

Ground cumin, 2¼ teaspoons

**Coarse kosher salt and
freshly ground pepper**

**Spaghetti, preferably
multigrain,** 10–12 oz
(315–375 g)

Olive oil, 2½ tablespoons

Large shallots, 3, minced

Corn kernels, cut from
3 ears, about 2 cups
(¾ lb/375 g)

Zucchini, 2, finely diced

Low-sodium beef broth,
1 cup (8 fl oz/250 ml)

Unsalted butter,
1½–2 tablespoons

Fresh marjoram, ¼ cup
(⅓ oz/10 g) minced, plus
leaves for garnish

makes 4 servings

● Rub the steak with 1¼ teaspoons paprika and 1¼ teaspoons cumin. Sprinkle lightly with salt and pepper.

● Bring a large pot three-fourths full of salted water to a boil. Add the pasta, stir well, and cook until al dente, about 11 minutes.

● Meanwhile, in a large frying pan over medium-high heat, warm 1 tablespoon of the oil. Add the steak and cook as desired, 3–4 minutes per side for medium-rare. Transfer to a warmed plate and cover with foil to keep warm.

● Add the remaining 1½ tablespoons oil to the pan. Add the shallots and sauté until fragrant, about 30 seconds. Add the corn kernels, zucchini, remaining 1 teaspoon paprika and 1 teaspoon cumin. Sprinkle with salt and pepper and sauté until the corn and zucchini are almost tender, about 3 minutes. Add the broth and boil until syrupy, about 2 minutes. Add the butter and stir until melted. Mix in ¼ cup (⅓ oz/10 g) minced marjoram.

● Drain the pasta and return it to the pot it was cooked in. Add the corn mixture and stir to coat. Taste and adjust the seasoning. Cut the steak thinly across the grain. Divide the pasta among 4 warmed plates. Top with the sliced steak. Sprinkle with marjoram leaves and serve right away.

quick tips

The sauce for the pasta comes together so quickly, it can be made while the spaghetti cooks. Top sirloin is a flavorful, economical cut of beef, but be certain to slice it thinly so it won't be tough. Boneless rib eye steak makes a luxurious substitute. Look for Spanish smoked paprika, or *pimentón*, in a specialty-food store; it is a great way to add lots of flavor with just one ingredient—one of my secrets to quick weeknight cooking.

Bell peppers, eggplant, and zucchini are all at their best in summer. Here they are simply grilled, then tossed with a vibrant mustard vinaigrette. Blue cheese and walnuts add richness, while chickpeas add protein to this plentiful salad.

tangy **summer vegetable salad** with bulgur

Dijon mustard,
1½ tablespoons

Sherry vinegar,
3 tablespoons

Large shallot, 1, minced

Extra-virgin olive oil, ½ cup
(4 fl oz/125 ml), plus more
as needed

Fresh flat-leaf parsley,
3 tablespoons minced, plus
torn leaves for garnish

**Coarse kosher salt and
freshly ground pepper**

Chickpeas, 1 can (15 oz/
470 g), rinsed and drained

Bulgur wheat, 1 cup
(6 oz/185 g)

Red bell peppers,
2, quartered lengthwise

Yellow bell peppers,
2, quartered lengthwise

Asian eggplants, 3, cut
lengthwise into thirds

Zucchini, 3, cut lengthwise
into thirds

Blue cheese, ½ cup
(2.5 oz/75 g) crumbled

Walnuts, coarsely chopped,
for garnish

makes 4 servings

Prepare a charcoal or gas grill for direct-heat cooking over high heat. In a small bowl, place the mustard. Mix in the vinegar, and then the shallot. Gradually whisk in ½ cup (4 fl oz/125 ml) of the oil. Add the minced parsley. Season the vinaigrette to taste with salt and pepper. In a large bowl, combine the chickpeas and half of the vinaigrette. Stir to coat. Taste and adjust the seasoning.

In a medium saucepan, combine the bulgur and 1½ cups (12 fl oz/375 ml) cold water. Season lightly with salt. Bring to a boil, and then reduce the heat to low. Cover and simmer until the bulgur is just tender, 12–15 minutes. Turn off the heat and let the bulgur stand, covered, for at least 5 minutes.

Meanwhile, brush the peppers, eggplants, and zucchini with olive oil, and then sprinkle with salt and pepper. Arrange the vegetables on the grill rack, cover, and cook until brown in spots, about 7 minutes per side. Transfer the vegetables to a cutting board, cut crosswise into thirds, and then slice lengthwise. Transfer to the bowl with the chickpeas. Add enough vinaigrette to season to taste and toss to coat.

Fluff the bulgur with a fork, and then spoon into a large shallow bowl. Top with the vegetables. Sprinkle with the cheese, walnuts, and a few parsley leaves and serve hot or at room temperature.

quick tips

Choose quick-cooking bulgur to keep the preparation time manageable on a weeknight. Grilling the vegetables keeps the kitchen cool in the summer, but broiling them works just as well. Other good vegetables to use in this salad include poblano chiles, Anaheim chiles, and radicchio. The dressing and bulgur can be made 1 day ahead and leftovers are great just as they are.

Cumin, coriander, cinnamon, and cayenne perk up everyday chicken thighs in this easy, Moroccan-inspired recipe. Serve it with boiled garden beans and whole-grain couscous flavored with lemon zest and cilantro.

spice-rubbed **grilled chicken**

Skinless, boneless chicken thighs, 1¼–1½ lb (625–750 g)

Olive oil, 1 tablespoon

Fresh lemon juice, 1 tablespoon

Coarse kosher salt and freshly ground pepper

Ground cumin, 1½ teaspoons

Ground coriander, ¾ teaspoon

Ground cinnamon, ¾ teaspoon

Cayenne pepper, ⅛–¼ teaspoon

Grated lemon zest, 1½ teaspoons

Fresh cilantro, minced

makes 4 servings

● Cut excess fat from the chicken. Place the chicken on a small baking sheet. Brush on both sides with olive oil and lemon juice, and sprinkle with salt and pepper. Mix the cumin, coriander, cinnamon, and cayenne in a small bowl, and then sprinkle over both sides of the chicken. Sprinkle with the lemon zest.

● Prepare a charcoal or gas grill for direct-heat grilling over high heat. Add the chicken to the grill rack, cover, and cook until springy to the touch and cooked through, about 6 minutes per side. Transfer the chicken to a warmed platter and sprinkle with cilantro. Serve right away.

quick tips

Boneless chicken thighs take only minutes to grill. If you are cooking for two, make the entire recipe, then cut up leftover chicken and vegetables and mix them into the remaining couscous; season the mixture with olive oil and vinegar for an easy dinner salad the next night. Cut-up cucumber, tomato, and radishes would be delicious additions. Toasted almonds or pine nuts would add pleasant crunch.

Clean Asian flavors—tangy lime juice, peppery ginger, and fresh herbs—offer bright contrast to the rich-tasting skewered beef. Serve with rice and steamed sugar-snap peas tossed with Asian sesame oil and toasted sesame seeds.

beef skewers with fresh lime–herb sauce

summer

Fresh lime juice, ¼ cup (2 fl oz/60 ml), plus lime wedges for garnish (optional)

Vegetable oil, 3 tablespoons

Low-sodium soy sauce, 1 tablespoon

Fresh ginger, ¼-inch (6-mm) piece about 1 inch (2.5 cm) in diameter, peeled and minced

Small shallot, 1, minced

Serrano chile, 1, seeded and minced

Sugar, 1 teaspoon

Skirt steak, 8–10 oz (250–315 g)

Fresh cilantro, 2 tablespoons minced

Fresh mint, 1 tablespoon minced

Coarse kosher salt and freshly ground pepper

Cooked rice, preferably brown jasmine or basmati

Green onions, 2, green parts, only, thinly sliced for serving (optional)

makes 2 servings; can be doubled

• Soak 8 bamboo skewers in water to cover for 30 minutes.

• Meanwhile, in a small bowl, combine the lime juice, 2 tablespoons of the oil, soy sauce, ginger, shallot, chile, sugar, and 2 tablespoons water; set aside. Cut the steak crosswise into segments 3 inches (7.5 cm) long, and then cut the segments in half lengthwise.

• In a medium bowl, place the steak. Stir the lime-soy mixture briefly, and then add 2 tablespoons to the steak. Add the remaining 1 tablespoon oil, and mix to coat the steak well. Let the steak marinate for 10–15 minutes. Mix the cilantro and mint into the remaining lime sauce.

• Prepare a charcoal or gas grill for direct-heat grilling over high heat. Thread 2 pieces of steak onto each skewer. Sprinkle with salt and pepper. Place the skewers on the grill and cook as desired, about 3 minutes per side for rare. Serve right away, passing the rice, lime sauce, green onions, if using, and lime wedges, if using, separately.

quick tips

Economical skirt steak is sliced a little thicker than usual for saté-style dishes. Make the marinade and dipping sauce a day ahead, if you like, or make extra to serve with shrimp, fish, or chicken.

Ground bison is a surprise ingredient in this burger recipe. Healthier than beef, it is low in saturated fat and high in omega-3 fatty acids. Marjoram adds a slightly floral flavor to the topping. Accompany with grilled corn and pickles.

buffalo burgers with tomato and marjoram topping

Olive oil, 4 teaspoons

Large onion, 1, finely chopped

Serrano chiles, 3, seeded and minced

Ground bison (buffalo), turkey, or beef, 1¼ lb (625 g)

Fresh marjoram, ¼ cup (⅓ oz/10 g) minced

Cherry tomatoes, ¾ lb (375 g), quartered, or 2 large tomatoes, chopped

Fresh lime juice

Coarse kosher salt and freshly ground pepper

makes 4 servings

• Prepare a charcoal or gas grill for direct-heat grilling over high heat.

• In a heavy small frying pan over medium heat, warm the oil. Add ¾ of the onion and 2 of the chiles and sauté until tender, about 5 minutes. In a medium bowl, place the meat. Add the onion mixture and ½ of the marjoram. Mix gently to blend. Form 4 patties 1 inch (2.5 cm) thick.

• Mix the tomatoes and the remaining ¼ onion, chile, and marjoram in a small bowl. Season to taste with lime juice, salt, and pepper.

• Sprinkle the burgers with salt and pepper. Grill as desired, about 3 minutes per side for rare (beads of juice will rise to the surface of bison burgers). Transfer to warmed plates, top with the tomato mixture, and serve right away.

quick tips

Because it is so low in fat, bison, also known as buffalo, benefits from being seasoned well—here I've used onion, chile, and herbs. It is also best cooked rare to preserve the natural juices. These patties can be made with ground beef or turkey and can be seasoned, formed, and refrigerated 1 day ahead of time. If you like, cilantro, thyme, or oregano could replace the marjoram.

Bright Asian seasonings such as ginger, lime, chile sauce, and fresh herbs help delicate tofu and rice shine in this satisfying vegetarian supper. Peanuts add richness and crunch. Sautéed shiitake mushrooms are a delicious addition.

asian-style **tofu, rice, and broccoli salad**

Coarse kosher salt

Brown basmati or jasmine rice, 1⅓ cups (9½ oz/295 g)

Fresh ginger, ¼ cup (1 oz/30 g) peeled and thinly sliced

Fresh lime juice, ¼ cup (2 fl oz/60 ml)

Low-sodium soy sauce or Asian fish sauce, 2 tablespoons

Chile sauce such as sriracha or sambal oelek, 1 tablespoon

Asian sesame oil, 2 teaspoons

Firm tofu, 14–16 oz (440–500 g), drained, patted dry, and cut into ½-inch (12-mm) cubes

Baby broccoli, broccoli rabe, or broccoli, 1½ lb (750 g)

Fresh cilantro, ½ cup (¾ oz/20 g) minced

Fresh mint, ½ cup (¾ oz/20 g) minced

Fresh basil, ½ cup (¾ oz/20 g) minced

Dry roasted peanuts, coarsely chopped for garnish

makes 4 servings

In a saucepan, bring 2 cups (16 fl oz/500 ml) salted water to a boil over high heat. Add the rice and return to a boil. Reduce the heat to low, cover, and cook for 30 minutes. Turn off the heat and let stand for 5 minutes. Fluff the rice with a fork, transfer to a large bowl, and cool.

Meanwhile, in the work bowl of a food processor, combine the ginger, lime juice, soy sauce, 2 tablespoons water, chile sauce, and sesame oil. Process until the ginger is finely minced. Transfer the mixture to a medium bowl. Mix in the tofu and let marinate while preparing the remaining ingredients.

If using baby broccoli or broccoli rabe, cut into 2-inch (5-cm) pieces. If using broccoli, peel the stalks by inserting the edge of a small sharp knife under the edge of the peel and pulling toward the florets. Cut the florets off the stems, and cut the stems into 2-inch (5-cm) pieces. In a steamer over boiling water, steam the vegetable until tender-crisp, about 3 minutes for baby broccoli or broccoli rabe, or about 6 minutes for broccoli florets and stems. Transfer the vegetables to a large bowl of cold water, let stand briefly to cool, and then drain well.

Cut the broccoli into bite-size pieces and add to the rice. Stir in the tofu mixture and herbs. Garnish with peanuts and serve right away.

quick tips

If you like, cook the rice the night before, cool it to room temperature, and refrigerate. You can also marinate the tofu in the seasonings overnight. Once mixed, the salad keeps well and could be enjoyed again on a subsequent night. Baby broccoli has a gentler flavor than regular broccoli, but either works well. Broccoli rabe would lend a slightly more assertive flavor. Cooked shrimp or leftover chicken would also be fine substitutes for the tofu.

Summer-fresh peaches accented with red onions, chopped fresh cilantro, and chipotle chiles make an original topping for lamb chops. Grilled summer squash makes a good accompaniment and rice would nicely round out the meal.

grilled lamb chops with fresh peach salsa

Lamb shoulder round bone chops, 2, each 1 inch (2.5 cm) thick

Ground cumin, ½ teaspoon

Ground cinnamon, ¼ teaspoon

Coarse kosher salt and freshly ground pepper

Olive oil for brushing

Peaches, 2 (12 oz/375 g total weight), peeled, if desired, and chopped

Red onion, 3 tablespoons minced

Fresh cilantro, 3 tablespoons roughly chopped

Canned chipotle chiles in adobo sauce, ½–1½ teaspoons minced with sauce

Fresh lime juice, 1 teaspoon

makes 2 servings;
can be doubled

● Rub both sides of the lamb chops with the cumin and cinnamon. Sprinkle with salt and pepper, and then brush with olive oil.

● In a small bowl, combine the peaches, red onion, cilantro, chiles, and lime juice. Season to taste with salt and pepper.

● Prepare a charcoal or gas grill for direct-heat grilling over high heat. Place the lamb on the grill rack. Cover the grill and cook the lamb for about 3½ minutes per side for medium-rare. Place 1 lamb chop on each plate. Drain the salsa and spoon on top of the lamb. Serve right away.

quick tips

Shoulder chops are an economical and very tasty cut of lamb, perfect for a busy weeknight. Look for chops with a round bone near one end, sometimes called shoulder arm chops. This recipe is also great with lamb loin chops, pork chops, or salmon fillets. If the peaches are excessively fuzzy, pull off the peel with a sharp knife. Or, blanch them in boiling water for 30 seconds, and then transfer to a bowl of cold water; the skins will slip off easily.

I like to give avocado a Japanese flavor profile with wasabi paste and fresh ginger. Here, it embellishes grilled turkey cutlets in an innovative sandwich. Serve it with a green salad and sweet potato chips.

turkey sandwiches with ginger-avocado relish

Green onions, 4, white and pale green parts minced

Olive oil, 2 tablespoons

Rice vinegar, 5 teaspoons

Fresh ginger, 3½ teaspoons peeled and minced

Wasabi paste, 2 teaspoons

Avocado, 1 firm but ripe, pitted, peeled, and diced

Coarse kosher salt and freshly ground pepper

Turkey breast cutlets, 1¼–1½ lb (625–750 g)

Asian sesame oil

Country bread, 4 thick slices

Butter lettuce, 4 large leaves, sliced

makes 4 servings

In a bowl, combine the green onions, olive oil, vinegar, 2 teaspoons of the minced ginger, and the wasabi. Gently mix in the avocado. Season to taste with salt and pepper; and set aside.

Prepare a charcoal or gas grill for direct-heat cooking over high heat. Brush the turkey with sesame oil on both sides, and sprinkle both sides with salt and pepper. Sprinkle the remaining 1½ teaspoons ginger over one side of the turkey. Brush sesame oil over one side of the bread. Grill the turkey until just cooked through, 2–3 minutes on each side. Transfer to a plate. Grill the bread, oiled side down, until golden brown, 2–3 minutes.

Arrange 1 bread slice, grilled side up, on each plate. Arrange sliced lettuce over each, and then top with turkey. Spoon the relish over and serve right away.

quick tips

Turkey cutlets are terrific for weeknight dinners because they cook quickly and taste great, but these sandwiches would also be delicious with grilled chicken breasts or fish fillets. Grilling punches up the flavors of the poultry, but if you don't feel like grilling, quickly sauté the turkey in a frying pan and toast the bread in a toaster. Look for wasabi paste in the Asian food section of the supermarket or in a specialty-food store.

112

I love how a quick and easy curry mixture perfumes chicken and vegetables, transforming their taste. A quick yogurt sauce highlights the Indian flavors. Accompany the meal with steamed rice and end with slices of fresh mango.

grilled chicken and vegetables with indian spices

Plain yogurt, ¾ cup
(6 oz/185 g)

Fresh cilantro, 3 tablespoons
minced

Green onions, 3, white and
pale green parts minced

**Coarse kosher salt and
freshly ground pepper**

Madras curry powder,
2 teaspoons

Chili powder, 2 teaspoons

Ground cumin, ½ teaspoon

Ground coriander,
½ teaspoon

**Skinless, boneless
chicken breast halves,**
4 (5–6 oz/155–185 g each)

Asian eggplants, 4, each cut
lengthwise into 3 pieces

Zucchini, 4, each cut
lengthwise into 3 pieces

Olive oil for brushing

makes 4 servings

• In a small bowl, combine the yogurt, cilantro, and green onions. Mix to blend. Season the yogurt sauce to taste with salt and pepper.

• Prepare a charcoal or gas grill for direct-heat cooking over high heat.

• In another small bowl, combine the curry powder, chile powder, cumin, and coriander. Mix to blend. Working with 1 chicken breast half at a time, place on a sheet of waxed paper, and then cover with a second sheet of waxed paper. Using a rolling pin, hit the chicken a few times to flatten slightly to an even thickness. Transfer the chicken to a rimmed baking sheet. Place the eggplant and zucchini on another baking sheet. Brush the top side of the chicken and vegetables with oil, and sprinkle with salt and pepper. Sprinkle the top of each chicken breast with ¼ teaspoon of the spice mixture, and then lightly sprinkle the vegetables with the spice mixture. Turn the chicken breasts and vegetables over and repeat brushing with the oil and seasonings (reserve any remaining spice mixture for another use).

• Place the chicken and vegetables on the grill. Cover and grill until just cooked through, about 5 minutes on each side for the chicken and eggplant, and about 6 minutes on each side for the zucchini.

• Transfer the chicken and vegetables to a platter. Serve with the yogurt sauce.

quick tips

Madras curry powder, found in the spice section of supermarkets, is a convenient way to add lots of flavor quickly. Use any leftover spice mixture to season poultry, fish, or vegetables, or make a quick sauce by stirring it into yogurt. For a change of pace, turkey cutlets or fish could stand in for the chicken; bell peppers and potatoes could replace the eggplant and zucchini.

fall is one of the best times of year for cooking. The summer vegetables are often still available and the autumn specialties are just coming to market.

fresh & fast meals for **fall**

Fall is a transitional season, and one of my favorites for cooking. The warm days of summer are waning, but often its bounty has not completely disappeared. On summer's heels I look forward to a plentiful harvest of sweet, golden-fleshed squash; wild mushrooms; an abundance of roots and tubers; and sturdy, mature greens such as kale and chard. Fall is the season that welcomes us back into the warmth of the kitchen. As you'll see in the pages that follow, I like to transform its offerings into nourishing soups and stews, hearty meat and poultry braises and roasts, and comforting pasta dishes.

fall market inspirations

- apples
- beets
- bell peppers
- broccoli
- brussels sprouts
- carrots
- caulaiflower
- chiles
- figs
- hard-shelled squash
- kale
- mushrooms, wild and cultivated
- parsnips
- pears
- potatoes
- spinach
- sweet potatoes
- swiss chard
- walnuts
- zucchini

add a simple side

- Wrap beets in foil and roast at 400°F (200°C) until tender, 1–1½ hours. Peel, cut into wedges, and toss with vinaigrette and fresh herbs

- Peel and grate carrots and toss with a mustard vinaigrette. Garnish with minced fresh parsley or chopped green onions

- Stir-fry blanched broccoli or cauliflower florets with minced garlic and red pepper flakes

- Roast whole sweet potatoes (prick them with a fork a few times first) in a 400°F (200°C) oven until tender, about 50 minutes, and serve with molasses- and allspice-flavored butter

choose fruit for dessert

- Cut firm but ripe pears into slices, then sauté with butter and maple syrup until tender and glazed; spoon over frozen yogurt

- Slice tart apples, preferably local fruit from a nearby farm, and serve with wedges of sharp Cheddar cheese and walnuts

- Cut ripe fresh figs in half, arrange in a baking dish, and bake in a 400°F (200°C) oven until tender and hot, 10–15 minutes; top with Greek yogurt mixed with Port and sugar to taste

smart strategies for fall meals

stock up on warming spices As the weather cools, I like to add spices that lend a warming sensation to my cooking. Ancho chile powder, nutmeg, allspice, paprika, garam masala, and turmeric are favorite additions to the heartier dishes of the season.

take advantage of Indian summer The early days of fall are often more like summer and, in warm years, the summer produce still proliferates in the markets. Take advantage by incorporating into your cooking the tomatoes, bell peppers, zucchini, and other summer vegetables that you will surely miss once they are gone.

tips for simmering and braising Slowly simmering foods on the stove top is ideal for many fall recipes, since the chilly weather calls for cozy soups, stews, and braised meats and poultry. For the best flavor, be sure to brown meat or poultry well before combining with other ingredients; this will impart a rich taste to the dish.

plan a second helping Given that soups, stews, and braises reheat well, make big batches and refrigerate or freeze leftovers for future meals. Often, they are better the second time around.

brown bag it In the spirit of back-to-school time, pack the remnants of last night's dinner for today's lunch. Or, freeze meals and store them for days or nights when there isn't time to cook.

Peppery pancetta, robust Italian tomatoes, and fresh thyme embellish this quick version of the traditionally long cooking sauce. I love it over egg pappardelle or fettuccine, served with a mixed greens salad alongside.

pappardelle with quick bolognese sauce

Olive oil, 1 tablespoon

Large onion, 1, finely chopped

Ground beef, 1 lb (500 g)

Pancetta, 2 oz (60 g),
finely chopped

**Coarse kosher salt and
freshly ground pepper**

Dry white wine,
½ cup (4 fl oz/125 ml)

**Whole tomatoes in juice,
preferably San Marzano,** 1 can
(14.28–14.5 oz/448–455 g)

Low-sodium chicken broth,
¾ cup (6 fl oz/180 ml)

Heavy cream, 1–2 tablespoons

Nutmeg, ⅛ teaspoon
freshly grated

**Dried egg pappardelle
or fettuccine,** 12 oz (375 g)

Fresh thyme, 1 tablespoon
minced

Parmesan cheese,
freshly grated, for serving

makes 4 servings

● In a large frying pan over medium heat, warm the oil. Add the onion and sauté until tender and it begins to brown, about 5 minutes. Increase the heat to medium-high, and add the ground beef and pancetta. Season with salt and pepper and sauté, breaking up the meat with a wooden spoon, just until the beef is no longer pink. Add the wine and boil until it has almost evaporated, about 3 minutes. Add the tomatoes with their juice, broth, cream, and nutmeg. Reduce the heat to medium-low and simmer, breaking up the tomatoes and stirring occasionally, until slightly thickened and the flavors are blended, about 30 minutes. Taste and adjust the seasoning.

● Meanwhile, bring a large pot three-fourths full of salted water to a boil. Add the pasta, stir well, and cook until just tender, about 8 minutes. Drain the pasta, and then return to the same pot. Add the sauce and toss to coat.

● Divide among 4 warmed shallow bowls. Sprinkle each with thyme and cheese. Serve right away, passing more cheese alongside.

quick tips

A touch of heavy cream replaces the milk usually used in Bolognese sauce; it lends a silky texture in a shorter cooking time. The sauce keeps well and is even richer in flavor when reheated, so make it a day or two ahead, or prepare extra to freeze. Spaghetti is another good pasta choice.

fall

Succulent white beans, sweet winter squash, and bright chard simmer together in this meatless main-course soup; it is the first soup I make every fall when the hard-shelled squashes appear at the market. Serve with hunks of hearty bread.

autumn **vegetable soup**

fall

Olive oil, 1 tablespoon

Large onion, 1, finely chopped

Red bell pepper, 1, chopped

Fresh rosemary,
1 tablespoon minced

Red pepper flakes,
¼ teaspoon

Hard-shelled squash such as butternut, 2 lb (1 kg), peeled, seeded, and cut into ¾-inch (2-cm) pieces

Coarse kosher salt and freshly ground black pepper

Low-sodium chicken broth,
4 cups (32 fl oz/1 l),
plus more as needed

Cannellini beans, 1 can
(15 oz/470 g), rinsed
and drained

Swiss chard, 1 bunch,
tough stems removed,
coarsely chopped

makes 4–6 servings

● In a large saucepan over medium heat, warm the oil. Add the onion, bell pepper, rosemary, and pepper flakes. Sauté until the onion and bell pepper are tender, about 12 minutes. Add the squash, sprinkle with salt and black pepper, and cook, stirring frequently, until the surface starts to soften, about 2 minutes. Add the 4 cups (32 fl oz/1 l) broth and the beans. Bring to a boil, reduce the heat, and simmer, stirring occasionally, until the squash is tender, about 25 minutes.

● Add the chopped chard and simmer until wilted, about 3 minutes. Thin the soup with more broth if desired. Taste and adjust the seasoning. Ladle into warmed bowls and serve right away.

quick tips

I make variations on this basic recipe all fall and winter, adding more broth for a thinner version, less for thicker; including sausages for a richer soup; and substituting different vegetables and beans depending on what I find at the market or have on hand. Leftover pasta, meat, or chicken adds great flavor. The tastes deepen each time this soup is reheated.

Fragrant seeds give the fish a crunchy coating as well as contribute exotic flavor. Sweet pears mixed with lime juice, fresh ginger, and spicy chile form a quick relish. I like to serve this easy dish with cooked rice and green beans.

spice-crusted tuna with fresh pear chutney

Albacore tuna steaks,
4, each about 6 oz (185 g)
and 1 inch (2.5 cm) thick

Coriander seeds,
2 teaspoons

Cumin seeds, 2 teaspoons

Lemon zest, 2 teaspoons
grated

**Coarse kosher salt and
freshly ground pepper**

Large Bosc pears, 2, firm
but ripe, finely diced

Fresh lime juice,
2 tablespoons

Fresh cilantro, 2 tablespoons
minced

Fresh ginger,
1 tablespoon peeled
and minced

Serrano chile, ½ teaspoon
seeded and minced

Olive oil, 1 teaspoon

makes 4 servings

● Place the tuna in a shallow baking pan. In a spice mill or mortar with pestle, coarsely grind the coriander and cumin seeds. Press the seeds into both sides of the tuna. Sprinkle both sides with the lemon zest, salt, and pepper. Set aside while making the chutney.

● In a bowl, combine the pears, lime juice, cilantro, ginger, and chile. Season the chutney to taste with salt and pepper.

● In a large nonstick frying pan over medium-high heat, warm the oil. Add the fish and cook as desired, 2–3 minutes per side for medium-rare.

● Place the fish on a platter or divide among 4 warmed plates. Spoon the chutney on top of the fish and serve right away.

quick tips

The fish cooks in about 6 minutes, which is about the same amount of time it takes to put together the quick chutney. To vary the dish, try salmon, tilapia, or halibut; apples could stand in for the pears. Any leftover fish can be cubed and heated in a tomato sauce for a fast pasta dinner the next night.

fall

This recipe is perfect when you have a glut of vegetables in your garden during Indian summer. I like to take advantage of the lingering warm weather by grilling the vegetables outdoors, but you can also cook them under the broiler.

pasta with ratatouille-style vegetables

Olive oil, 2 tablespoons, plus more as needed

Large onion, 1, finely chopped

Red bell pepper, 1, thinly sliced, slices cut crosswise in thirds

Yellow bell pepper, 1, thinly sliced, slices cut crosswise in thirds

Fresh thyme, 2 teaspoons minced

Red pepper flakes

Coarse kosher salt and freshly ground black pepper

Italian tomatoes, preferably San Marzano, 1 can (28 oz/875 g)

Dry white wine, ¾ cup (6 fl oz/180 ml)

Sugar, pinch (optional)

Asian eggplants, 2, cut lengthwise into thirds

Zucchini, 2, cut lengthwise into thirds

Fresh basil, ¼ cup (⅓ oz/ 10 g) chopped

Rotini or fusilli pasta, preferably multigrain, 12 oz (375 g)

Fresh goat cheese, crumbled

makes 4 servings

● In a large frying pan over medium heat, warm the 2 tablespoons oil. Add the onion, bell peppers, thyme, and a pinch of pepper flakes; sprinkle with salt and black pepper. Sauté until the peppers are tender, about 15 minutes. Add the tomatoes with their juices, and break them up with a spoon. Add the wine and simmer to blend flavors, 15–20 minutes, stirring frequently. Taste and adjust the seasoning, adding a pinch of sugar if the sauce tastes too acidic.

● Prepare a charcoal or gas grill for direct-heat grilling over medium-high heat, or preheat the broiler. Arrange the eggplant and zucchini on a rimmed baking sheet, brush on both sides with olive oil; sprinkle with salt and pepper. Transfer to the grill rack, cover, and grill until tender, about 5 minutes per side. Or broil until tender, about 5 minutes per side. Cut the eggplant and zucchini into bite-size pieces and add to the sauce. Add the basil.

● Meanwhile, bring a large pot three-fourths full of salted water to a boil. Add the pasta, stir well, and cook until al dente, about 11 minutes. Drain the pasta, and then add to the sauce and toss to coat. Transfer to a warmed large shallow bowl. Sprinkle generously with cheese and serve right away.

quick tips

Canned San Marzano tomatoes from Italy, available in many supermarkets and at Italian delis, add appealing sweetness to the sauce. Buy a few cans to have on hand for unplanned meals. This pasta dish reheats well; put leftovers in a frying pan, add a little water, cover, and cook, stirring occasionally, until the ingredients are heated through.

fall

This recipe is a cross between bruschetta and an open-faced sandwich. The meat is seasoned with peppercorns and thyme, then topped with a creamy and piquant shallot–Dijon mustard sauce. Serve with a lettuce and tomato salad.

steak sandwiches with shallot-thyme aioli

Whole peppercorns,
2 teaspoons

Fresh thyme, 4 teaspoons,
plus 1 tablespoon minced

Coarse kosher salt

Top round or flank steak,
1¼ lb (625 g), 1 inch
(2.5 cm) thick

Mayonnaise,
⅓ cup (3 fl oz/80 ml)

Large shallot, 1, minced

Extra-virgin olive oil,
1½ tablespoons

**Sherry vinegar or
fresh lemon juice,**
1 tablespoon

Dijon mustard, ¾ teaspoon

Freshly ground pepper

Olive oil for brushing

Coarse country white bread,
8–12 slices

Watercress, 1 bunch

makes 4 servings

In a spice mill or mortar with pestle, coarsely grind the peppercorns. Mix with the 4 teaspoons thyme and 2 teaspoons salt. Pat the steak dry. Press the spice mixture onto both sides of the meat, and let marinate while preparing the aioli.

In a small bowl, combine the mayonnaise, shallot, oil, vinegar or lemon juice, mustard, remaining 1 tablespoon thyme, and freshly ground pepper; mix to combine. Set the aioli aside.

In a heavy large frying pan over medium-high heat, brush with olive oil. Add the steak and cook as desired, about 4 minutes per side for medium-rare. Transfer to a plate and let rest 5 minutes.

Meanwhile, preheat the broiler. Brush one side of each bread slice with a little of the aioli. Arrange, aioli side up, on a baking sheet and broil until brown, watching carefully, about 2 minutes. Place 2–3 bread slices on each of 4 warmed plates. Spread each with aioli, and then top with watercress.

Thinly slice the steak on an angle against the grain. Arrange the meat on top of the watercress and serve right away.

quick tips

I like to use economical beef cuts for this recipe like top round or flank steak, but for a splurge, you can use New York strip, rib eye, or filet mignon. Make extra of the easy sauce to use on potato salad or as a dip for vegetables. It would also be great with simply broiled fish.

fall

A quartet of familiar spices lend the striking flavors of Morocco to this complete meal in one. Although it takes a bit longer than other recipes to cook, once you put it in the oven, your work is done. Purchased baklava is the perfect ending.

chicken and fall vegetables with moroccan flavors

fall

Chicken, 1 (5 lb/2.5 kg)

Coarse kosher salt and freshly ground black pepper

Sweet paprika, 2 tablespoons, plus 1½ teaspoons

Ground cumin, 1½ teaspoons

Red pepper flakes, ¾ teaspoon

Ground cinnamon, ¾ teaspoon

Lemon, 1

Olive oil, 5 tablespoons (3 fl oz/ 80 ml)

Small orange-fleshed sweet potatoes, 2 (about ¾ lb/375 g total weight), unpeeled

Cauliflower, 1 lb (500 g), cut into 1-inch (2.5-cm) florets

Red onion, 1, cut into 8 wedges

makes 4 servings

Preheat the oven to 450°F (230°C). Grease a heavy large rimmed baking sheet (not a roasting pan). Pull out and discard the fat and giblets from the main cavity in the chicken. Pat the chicken very dry with paper towels. Starting at the edge of the main cavity, slide a finger under the skin over each breast half, making pockets. Rub 1 tablespoon salt all over the chicken and in the main cavity. Sprinkle generously with black pepper. Tie the legs together, if desired.

In a small bowl, mix the paprika, cumin, pepper flakes, and cinnamon. Set aside 2½ teaspoons of the spice mixture for the vegetables. Finely grate the zest from the lemon, cut the lemon into quarters, and mix the zest into the remaining spices. Gradually mix in 2 tablespoons of the olive oil to make a paste. Spread a little of the paste inside the main cavity and under the skin over the breasts; rub the rest of the paste all over the outside of the chicken. Insert the lemon quarters into the main cavity. Place the chicken in the center of the prepared pan. Place the chicken in the oven and roast for 30 minutes.

Meanwhile, cut the sweet potatoes in half crosswise; quarter each piece lengthwise, forming wedges. Combine the sweet potatoes, cauliflower, and onion in a bowl. Add the remaining 3 tablespoons oil and toss to coat. Add the reserved spice mixture. Sprinkle with ½ teaspoon each salt and pepper, and toss to coat.

After the chicken has roasted for 30 minutes, remove it from the oven. Tilt the sheet pan and spoon off most of the fat. Arrange the chicken in the center of the pan and spoon the vegetables around the bird. Return the pan to the oven and continue roasting until an instant-read thermometer inserted into the thickest part of a thigh registers 165°F (74°C), about 40 minutes longer. (Note: the bird will take longer to roast if the legs have been tied together). If the skin is getting too dark, reduce the oven temperature to 425°F (220°C).

Transfer the chicken to a warmed decorative pan or platter and let rest for 10 minutes. Carve the chicken and serve right away with the vegetables.

Mahi mahi is an inexpensive, wild ocean fish that is harvested young, so mercury is not a concern. Here, I've topped it with a zesty olive-caper-lemon mixture. Serve it with olive oil–mashed potatoes and wilted greens.

roasted mahi mahi with olives, capers, and lemon

Extra-virgin olive oil,
1 tablespoon, plus more
as needed

Mahi mahi fillets, 2 (about
6–7 oz/185–220 g each)

**Coarse kosher salt and
freshly ground pepper**

Pitted kalamata olives,
⅓ cup (2 oz/60 g) chopped

Shallot, 1, minced

Capers, 1½ tablespoons

Fresh lemon juice,
1½ tablespoons

Grated lemon zest,
1 teaspoon

makes 2 servings

● Preheat the oven to 425°F (220°C). Brush a small glass baking dish with olive oil. Sprinkle the fish fillets on both sides with salt and pepper, place in the dish, and brush with oil on both sides.

● In a small bowl, combine the olives, shallot, capers, lemon juice and zest, and the 1 tablespoon oil; spoon the mixture over the fish. Roast the fish until just cooked through, about 12 minutes.

● Divide the fish and topping between warmed plates, spooning any drippings over the top. Serve right away.

quick tips

This dish is easy, yet elegant enough for a dinner party. You can easily double or triple it, selecting a roasting pan or two to accommodate all the fillets in a single layer. For convenience when entertaining, the olive topping can be made ahead and chilled. Keep olives and capers on hand to spruce up simple pasta sauces and sautéed vegetables.

fall

This rich-tasting chili is inspired by Mexican mole. Spicy andouille sausage is a clever replacement for beef. Serve with cornbread and jicama slices sprinkled with lime juice and chile powder. Finish with sugar cookies and lime sorbet.

mole-style chili with black beans and andouille

Olive oil, 1 tablespoon

Large onion, 1, finely chopped

Chicken or pork andouille sausages, 2 (about 6 oz/ 185 g total), finely diced

Zucchini, 3, cut into ½-inch (12-mm) pieces

Ground cumin, 1 teaspoon

Ancho chile powder, 1 teaspoon

Coarse kosher salt and freshly ground pepper

Diced tomatoes, 2 cans (14½ oz/455 g each)

Canned chipotle chiles in adobo sauce, 2 tablespoons minced with 1 tablespoon sauce

Unsweetened chocolate, 1 oz (30 g), finely chopped

Dried oregano, 1 teaspoon

Black beans, 2 cans (15 oz/470 g each), rinsed and drained

makes 4–6 servings

In heavy large pot over medium heat, warm the oil. Add the onion and sauté until it begins to soften, about 5 minutes. Add the sausages and cook until brown, about 5 minutes. Add the zucchini, cumin, and chile powder. Season with salt and pepper, and stir for 1 minute to toast the spices. Add the tomatoes with their juices, chipotle chiles, adobo sauce, chocolate, and oregano. Bring the chili to a boil, reduce the heat, and simmer 10 minutes to blend flavors.

Add the black beans to the pot and simmer until the zucchini is tender and the flavors have blended, thinning the chili with water if it is too thick, about 10 minutes longer.

Taste and adjust the seasonings with salt and pepper. Spoon the chili into warmed bowls and serve right away.

quick tips

Chipotle and ancho chile powder offer great flavor to recipes; keep them on hand for spicing quick-cooking recipes with little effort. Chipotle chiles in adobo sauce are available in cans in the Latin section of most markets. For a meatless version, leave out the sausage. This chili improves overnight, so make it one day ahead, or look forward to the leftovers.

Lamb patties are as appealing as beef, particularly when seasoned with cumin and allspice. Spoon gently spiced creamy yogurt sauce on top, then add the last of the summer tomatoes. Serve with chips and a vegetable salad.

lamb burgers with red onion–cumin sauce

Plain whole-milk yogurt,
½ cup (4 oz/125 g)

Red onion, ¾ cup
(3¾ oz/110 g) finely chopped

Ground cumin, ½ teaspoon

Cayenne pepper, pinch

**Coarse kosher salt and
freshly ground black pepper**

Ground lamb, 1¼ lb (625 g)

Ground allspice, ¾ teaspoon

Pita bread rounds, 6 inches
(15 cm) in diameter, 4, or
4 hamburger buns

Olive oil as needed

Tomato, 1, sliced

Baby spinach leaves
for serving

makes 4 servings

● In a small bowl, mix the yogurt, ⅓ of the onion, the cumin, and a pinch of cayenne. Season to taste with salt and black pepper. Set the sauce aside.

● In a medium bowl, combine the lamb, allspice, remaining onion, 1 teaspoon salt, and a generous amount of black pepper; mix gently to blend. Form the lamb mixture into 4 patties, each ½ inch (12 mm) thick. Heat a large frying pan over medium-high heat; brush with oil. Add the lamb patties and cook until done as desired, about 5 minutes per side for medium.

● Meanwhile, if using buns, preheat the broiler. Brush the cut surface of the buns with oil. Then broil, cut side up, until beginning to brown, about 2 minutes.

● If using pita bread, cut about ½ inch (12 mm) off one side of each round; place a patty in each pocket. If using buns, place one bun bottom on each of 4 warmed plates. Top each with a patty. Spoon some of the yogurt sauce over each patty, then top with a couple slices of tomato and a few spinach leaves. Serve right away, passing additional sauce at the table.

quick tips

Both the lamb patties and sauce can be made a day ahead; cover and refrigerate them until it's time to cook. The yogurt sauce is also good spooned over chicken or as a dressing for potato salad. Serve the patties tucked into either pita bread or hamburger buns.

fall

I discovered pasta with porcini and sausage sauce during my early days at *Bon Appétit* magazine, and I continue to adore the sensuous combination. Start with a shaved fennel salad topped with extra-virgin olive oil and Parmesan.

penne with mushrooms and turkey sausage

Dried porcini mushrooms,
¾ oz (20 g)

Olive oil, 1 tablespoon

Onion, 1, finely chopped

Hot Italian turkey sausages,
¾ lb (375 g), casings removed

Button mushrooms,
10–12 oz (315–375 g),
wiped clean and sliced

Fresh rosemary,
1 teaspoon chopped

**Coarse kosher salt and
freshly ground pepper**

Dry white wine,
⅓ cup (3 fl oz/80 ml)

Bay leaf, 1

Low-sodium chicken broth,
¾ cup (6 fl oz/180 ml), plus
more as needed

**Penne pasta,
preferably multigrain,**
12 oz (375 g)

Parmesan cheese, 1 cup
(4 oz/125 g) freshly grated,
plus more as needed

Fresh flat-leaf parsley,
chopped, for garnish

makes 4 servings

● Place the porcini mushrooms in a fine-mesh sieve, and rinse well. Transfer the porcini to a small bowl. Pour ¾ cup (6 fl oz/180 ml) hot water over and let soak until softened, about 20 minutes. Drain the porcini, reserving the soaking liquid. Chop the porcini, discarding any hard stems.

● In a heavy, very large frying pan over medium heat, warm the olive oil. Add the onion and cook until it begins to soften, stirring occasionally, about 5 minutes. Add the sausage, increase the heat to high, and cook until no longer pink, breaking up with a fork, about 4 minutes. Add the button mushrooms and rosemary, then season with salt and pepper. Stir until the mushrooms begin to soften, about 5 minutes. Add the porcini, wine, and bay leaf and boil until almost all the liquid evaporates, about 4 minutes. Add the ¾ cup (6 fl oz/180 ml) broth and the porcini soaking liquid and simmer, stirring occasionally, until the mixture becomes syrupy, about 10 minutes.

● Meanwhile, bring a large pot three-fourths full of salted water to a boil. Add the pasta, stir well, and cook until al dente, about 11 minutes. Drain the pasta and add to the pan with the sauce. Stir until the sauce coats the pasta. Remove from the heat; stir in the 1 cup (4 oz/125 g) cheese. Taste and adjust the seasoning.

● Transfer the pasta to warmed individual bowls or a large warmed serving bowl. Garnish with the parsley. Serve right away, passing additional cheese separately.

quick tips

I like to use turkey sausage when I want to keep things light. But for a little extra indulgence, pork sausage can replace the turkey. The sauce can be made a day ahead and then reheated before adding the pasta and cheese.

This recipe is a great way to breathe new life into predictable chicken breasts. Here, the crisp chicken sits on baby spinach and is drizzled with a rich tahini sauce, spiced with lemon and green onions. Finish with seasonal fresh fruit.

breaded chicken with lemon–green onion tahini

Tahini, ¼ cup (2½ oz/75 g)

Fresh lemon juice, 2 tablespoons, plus 1 teaspoon

Green onions, 3, white and green parts finely chopped

Coarse kosher salt and freshly ground pepper

Boneless, skinless chicken breast halves, 4 (5–6 oz/155–185 g each)

Large egg, 1

Dijon mustard, 2 teaspoons

Grated lemon zest, 1 teaspoon

Panko (Japanese bread crumbs), 1 cup (1½ oz/45 g)

Olive oil, 3 tablespoons

Baby spinach, 6 oz (185 g)

makes 4 servings

● In a small bowl, place the tahini. Mix in the 2 tablespoons of the lemon juice, and then mix in 2 tablespoons hot water. If needed, mix in more water to thin the mixture to the texture of thick mayonnaise. Mix in ⅔ of the green onions. Season the sauce to taste with salt and pepper.

● Place the chicken breast halves between 2 sheets of waxed paper; using a meat mallet or rolling pin, pound the breasts to a thickness of ⅓–½ inch (9–12 mm). In a bowl, combine the egg, remaining ⅓ of the green onions, the mustard, and lemon zest. Mix with a fork. Add the chicken and turn to coat. Sprinkle the chicken with salt and pepper. In a pie plate or cake pan, spread out the panko.

● In a large nonstick frying pan over medium-high heat, warm 2 tablespoons of the oil. Dip the chicken in panko, turning to coat on both sides, and then add to the pan. Cook until brown and cooked through, about 4 minutes per side.

● Meanwhile, place the spinach in a large bowl. Add the remaining 1 tablespoon oil and toss to coat. Season to taste with salt and pepper. Mix in the remaining 1 teaspoon lemon juice. Divide the spinach among 4 plates. Slice the chicken breast halves crosswise and place one breast half on top of the spinach on each plate. Spoon the tahini sauce over the top and serve right away.

fall

quick tips

Make extra sauce to use as a dip for vegetables or pita wedges another night. It's also delicious as a sauce for fish. Tahini, a peanut butter–like like paste made from ground sesame seeds, is available near the peanut butter in some supermarkets, at natural food stores, and in Middle Eastern stores. Stir it thoroughly before using. Panko, Japanese bread crumbs, are terrific for quick breading and are available where Asian food is sold.

Curry spices flatter chickpeas, cauliflower, and potatoes alike. Serve this zesty meatless dish over brown basmati or jasmine rice. I like to begin with sliced cucumbers seasoned with salt and fresh mint, and end with pistachio ice cream.

chickpea, cauliflower, and potato **curry**

Olive oil, 1 tablespoon

Large onion, 1, finely chopped

Serrano chiles, 2, chopped

Fresh ginger, 6-inch (15-cm) piece about 1 inch (2.5 cm) in diameter, peeled and minced

Cumin seeds, 1 teaspoon

Chickpeas, 2 cans (15 oz/ 470 g each) with liquid

Diced tomatoes, 1 can (14.5 oz/455 g)

Fresh lime juice, 1 tablespoon

Garam masala, ¾ teaspoon

Ground turmeric, rounded ¼ teaspoon

Large cauliflower, ½ head, cut into 1-inch (2.5-cm) florets

Yukon gold potatoes, 2, cut into ½-inch (12-mm) pieces

Coarse kosher salt and freshly ground pepper

Cooked rice for serving (optional)

Fresh cilantro, ⅓ cup (½ oz/ 15 g) minced

makes 4 servings

● In a heavy large saucepan over medium-high heat, warm the oil. Add the onion, chiles, ginger, and cumin seeds. Sauté until the onion is tender, about 6 minutes. Add the chickpeas with their liquid, tomatoes with their juice, lime juice, ½ teaspoon of the garam masala, and turmeric. Bring to a boil, and then reduce the heat and simmer for 5 minutes to blend the flavors.

● Add the cauliflower, potatoes, and 1 cup (8 fl oz/250 ml) water, and simmer until the potatoes are tender, stirring occasionally and adding more water if dry, about 15 minutes. Stir in the remaining ¼ teaspoon garam masala. Season to taste with salt and pepper.

● Divide the rice, if using, among 4 warmed shallow bowls. Spoon the curry over the top, sprinkle with cilantro, and serve right away.

quick tips

Garam masala, an aromatic Indian spice blend, can be found in the spice section of most supermarkets. It's a terrific seasoning to have on hand in the cupboard to add flavor to chicken, fish, potatoes, and sweet potatoes. This stew reheats well, so it can be served again a night or two later. Canned chickpeas are a versatile staple; they are great in salads, stews, and soups.

Inspired by the classic veal Marsala, this recipe features turkey cutlets, which go perfectly with the slightly sweet wine and earthy mushrooms. I serve this over bulgur wheat, which absorbs the sauce and adds great texture to the dish.

turkey cutlets with mushrooms and marsala

Turkey breast cutlets,
1¼ lb (625 g)

Coarse kosher salt and freshly ground pepper

Olive oil, 2½ tablespoons or more as needed

All-purpose flour for dredging

Large shallot, 1, minced

Button or cremini mushrooms, 1 lb (500 g), sliced

Dry Marsala, 1 cup (8 fl oz/250 ml)

Low-sodium chicken broth, ¾ cup (6 fl oz/180 ml)

Fresh thyme, 3 tablespoons minced

Unsalted butter, 1–2 tablespoons

Bulgur wheat, 1¼ cups (7.5 oz/235 g), cooked

makes 4 servings

Sprinkle the turkey on both sides with salt and pepper. In a 12-inch (30-cm) nonstick frying pan over medium-high heat, warm 1 tablespoon of the oil. Dredge half the turkey in the flour, shaking off excess, and add to the frying pan. Cook until just brown, about 2 minutes on each side. Transfer to a platter. Repeat with the remaining turkey, adding more oil to the frying pan if necessary.

Add 1½ tablespoons oil to the same frying pan, and then add the shallot. Sauté until fragrant, about 30 seconds. Add the mushrooms, sprinkle lightly with salt and pepper, and sauté until the mushroom juices are absorbed, about 4 minutes. Add the Marsala and broth and boil until the juices reduce and thicken slightly, about 8 minutes. Add the thyme and butter and stir until the butter dissolves. Add the turkey and any juices on the platter. Simmer, turning the turkey occasionally, until the sauce thickens slightly, about 3 minutes.

Divide the bulgur among 4 warmed plates. Arrange the turkey atop the bulgur. Spoon the mushrooms and sauce over the turkey and serve right away.

quick tips

Chicken cutlets work as well here as the turkey—both are perfect for quick sautéing. If you have it on hand, sweet Marsala can replace the dry, yielding a more syrupy sauce. On a busy night, use already sliced mushrooms to help make this recipe even easier.

fall

White beans simmered with pancetta, rosemary, and fire-roasted tomatoes make an enticing base for poached eggs. It's a novel choice for dinner and just as good for breakfast or lunch. Serve with thick slices of broiled country bread.

poached eggs with white bean–tomato ragout

fall

Olive oil, 1 tablespoon

Pancetta, 3 oz (90 g), chopped

Large onion, 1, finely chopped

Fresh rosemary, 4 teaspoons minced

Red pepper flakes, ¼–½ teaspoon

Fire-roasted tomatoes, 2 cans (14.5 oz/455 g each)

Cannellini beans, 2 cans (15 oz/470 g each), rinsed and drained

Coarse kosher salt and freshly ground pepper

White vinegar, 1–2 teaspoons

Large eggs, 4–8

Sharp Cheddar cheese, freshly grated

makes 4 servings

● In a large saucepan over medium heat, warm the oil. Add the chopped pancetta and sauté until it starts to brown, about 3 minutes. Add the onion, rosemary, and red pepper flakes, and sauté until the onion is tender, about 5 minutes. Add the tomatoes with their juices and the beans. Mix in ¾ cup (6 fl oz/180 ml) water. Bring to a boil, reduce the heat, and simmer until the mixture thickens and the flavors blend, about 15 minutes. Season to taste with salt and black pepper.

● Meanwhile, pour water into 1 (for 4 eggs) or 2 (for 8 eggs) large frying pans to the depth of 1 inch (2.5 cm). Season the water with salt and add 1 teaspoon vinegar for each frying pan. Bring the liquid to a boil, and then reduce the heat to maintain a bare simmer. One at a time, break an egg into a small cup, and then gently slip into the water. Simmer gently until the eggs are cooked as desired, 3–4 minutes for runny yolks or up to 5 minutes for firmer yolks.

● Divide the white bean mixture among 4 warmed bowls. Using a slotted spoon, transfer 1 or 2 eggs to each bowl. Top the eggs with grated cheese and black pepper and serve right away.

quick tips

For a meatless version, leave out the pancetta. The bean ragout makes a delicious side dish for chicken, lamb, or pork. Almost any grating cheese would be good here—Manchego, Parmesan, pecorino, and Comté are all excellent alternatives for the Cheddar. Fire-roasted canned tomatoes are a flavorful convenience item to keep on hand in the pantry.

Chard stirred into the rice-shaped pasta provides a vegetable component to this risotto-like dish, transforming it into the perfect base for quickly browned sea scallops. The quick pan sauce gains bright flavors from sherry vinegar.

seared scallops with greens and orzo

Olive oil, 2 tablespoons

Onion, ½, finely chopped

Orzo, 1 cup (7 oz/220 g)

Low-sodium chicken broth,
3 cups (24 fl oz/750 ml),
plus 3 tablespoons

**Greens such as red chard,
black kale, or escarole,**
1 cup (2 oz/60 g) chopped

Fresh flat-leaf parsley,
3 tablespoons minced

Fresh thyme, 3½ teaspoons
minced

Grated lemon zest,
1 teaspoon

**Coarse kosher salt and
freshly ground pepper**

Unsalted butter,
2 tablespoons

Large sea scallops, ¾ lb
(375 g)

Sherry vinegar,
3 tablespoons

makes 2 servings

● In a heavy saucepan over medium heat, warm 1 tablespoon of the oil. Add the onion and sauté until tender, about 5 minutes. Add the orzo and stir until it begins to brown, about 4 minutes. Add the 3 cups (24 fl oz/750 ml) broth and bring to a boil, stirring up the browned bits. Reduce the heat to medium-low and simmer until the orzo is almost tender, stirring frequently, about 15 minutes. Add the chard and stir until the orzo is tender, the greens have wilted, and the mixture is creamy, about 3 minutes. Mix in the parsley, 1½ teaspoons of the thyme, and the lemon zest. Season the orzo to taste with salt and pepper. Mix in 1 tablespoon of the butter. Remove from the heat, cover, and keep warm.

● Season the scallops on both sides with salt, pepper, and 1 teaspoon of the thyme. In a large frying pan over medium-high heat, warm the remaining 1 tablespoon oil. Add the scallops and sauté until almost springy to the touch, about 1½ minutes per side. Transfer the scallops to a warmed plate. Pour off the oil from the frying pan. Add the vinegar and remaining 3 tablespoons of broth to the frying pan and boil until syrupy, stirring up the browned bits, about 30 seconds. Remove the pan from the heat. Add any scallop juices from the plate. Swirl in the remaining 1 tablespoon of butter. Taste and adjust the seasoning.

● Divide the orzo mixture between 2 warmed plates. Top with the scallops; drizzle the pan sauce over the top, and then sprinkle with the remaining 1 teaspoon thyme. Serve right away.

fall

quick tips

Red chard lends a festive color to the dish, but any cooking greens will work well. The sophisticated, but simple recipe can be easily doubled to serve company; cooking the orzo with a technique used to prepare risotto gives it a luxurious, creamy texture. Store orzo and low-sodium chicken broth in the pantry—they are both great for quick-cooking meals.

Fresh rosemary, spicy pancetta, rich olives, and tart capers turn a simple stew into a popular weeknight meal. Use a mixture of red and yellow peppers for color, and spoon the stew over bulgur wheat or rice to complete the meal.

fall

braised chicken with peppers, olives, and capers

Chicken, 1 (about 3½ lb/ 1.75 kg), cut into 10 pieces

Coarse kosher salt and freshly ground black pepper

Olive oil, 1 tablespoon

Fresh rosemary, 2 tablespoons minced

Large red or yellow bell peppers, 2, sliced

Large onion, 1, halved and then sliced

Pancetta, 1½ oz (45 g), chopped

Red pepper flakes, ½ teaspoon

Diced tomatoes, 1 can (14½ oz/455 g)

Dry white wine, 1 cup (8 fl oz/250 ml)

Pitted kalamata olives, ⅓ cup (2 oz/60 g)

Capers, 2 tablespoons, rinsed

makes 4 servings

● Pat dry the chicken. Sprinkle on both sides with salt and black pepper. In a heavy large pot over medium-high heat, warm the oil. Add the rosemary, then the chicken pieces, in batches if necessary. Cook until brown, about 5 minutes on each side. Transfer to a plate.

● Add the bell peppers, onion, pancetta, and pepper flakes to the pot. Sprinkle with salt and black pepper, and sauté until they begin to soften, about 5 minutes. Add the tomatoes with their juice, wine, olives, and capers. Bring to a boil. Return the chicken to the pot. Reduce the heat to low, cover, and simmer until the breasts are just cooked, about 20 minutes. Transfer the breasts to a plate. Cover and cook the dark meat 10 minutes longer. Uncover and simmer until the dark meat is tender and the sauce has thickened slightly, about 15 minutes longer. Return the breasts to the sauce and simmer to heat through.

● Divide the chicken and sauce among 4 warmed plates and serve right away.

quick tips

Organic chickens have a purer flavor than their nonorganic counterparts. Using a sturdy large knife or cleaver, cut each breast in half crosswise so each person can have 1 piece of white meat and 1 piece of dark meat. For a new meal the next day, cut the leftover chicken meat into bite-size pieces, return it to the sauce, reheat gently, and mix it into hot, cooked pasta.

Ground lamb and zucchini cooked with fresh rosemary and tomatoes creates a succulent—and unexpected—sauce for pasta. Slightly salty pecorino cheese is the perfect garnish. End the meal with fresh grapes and sliced ripe pears.

pasta with lamb and rosemary

Olive oil, 2 tablespoons

Large onion, 1, thinly sliced

Fresh rosemary,
1 tablespoon minced

Ground lamb, ½ lb (500 g)

**Coarse kosher salt and
freshly ground pepper**

Dry white wine, ¼ cup
(2 fl oz/60 ml)

Diced tomatoes, 2 cans
(14.5 oz/455 g each)

Large zucchini, 2 (about
1 lb/500 g total), cut into
½-inch (12-mm) cubes

**Rotini or rotelle pasta,
preferably multigrain,**
10–12 oz (315–375 g)

Romano cheese, ½ cup
(2 oz/60 g) grated, plus
more as needed

makes 4 servings

In a large frying pan over medium-high heat, warm the oil. Add the onion and rosemary and sauté until the onion is tender, about 5 minutes. Add the lamb and sprinkle with salt and pepper. Sauté until the lamb is no longer pink, breaking up the meat with a wooden spoon, about 3 minutes. Add the wine and boil until absorbed, about 2 minutes. Add the tomatoes with their juice, and bring to a boil. Mix in the zucchini. Reduce the heat to medium-low and boil slowly until the sauce is thick, stirring occasionally, about 10 minutes.

Meanwhile, bring a large pot three-fourths full of salted water to a boil. Add the pasta, stir well, and cook until al dente, about 11 minutes. Drain the pasta, and then add to the sauce and toss to coat. Mix in the ½ cup (2 oz/60 g) cheese.

Taste and adjust the seasoning. Transfer to warmed shallow bowls. Serve right away, passing more cheese at the table.

quick tips

Lamb is wonderful with rosemary, but basil would be an equally delicious and slightly unusual addition; sprinkle in about 3 tablespoons chopped fresh basil when adding the cheese. Feta cheese would also be good with the lamb, lending a Greek flavor profile to the dish. The sauce can be made ahead and refrigerated. Reheat gently before serving.

fall

An easy glaze made from molasses, mustard, and fresh rosemary coat both the pork and sweet potatoes in this cozy supper. Sauté greens or steam broccoli to serve alongside. End the meal with warm gingerbread or ginger cookies.

molasses-glazed **roast pork and sweet potatoes**

Pork tenderloins, 2 (about 10–12 oz/315–375 g each)

Coarse kosher salt and freshly ground black pepper

Light molasses, ¼ cup (2.5 oz/75 g)

Dijon mustard, ¼ cup (2 oz/60 g)

Fresh rosemary, 1 tablespoon minced

Red pepper flakes, 1 teaspoon

Orange-fleshed sweet potatoes, 1½ lb (750 g), unpeeled, cut into ½-inch (12-mm) slices

Olive oil, 2½ tablespoons, plus more for brushing

Shallot, 1, minced

Low-sodium chicken broth, ½ cup (4 fl oz/125 ml)

makes 4 servings

fall

• Preheat the oven to 400°F (200°C). Sprinkle the outside of the pork lightly with salt and black pepper and set aside.

• In a small bowl, combine the molasses, mustard, rosemary, and ½ of the pepper flakes; stir to combine. In a large bowl, combine the sliced sweet potatoes, remaining ½ teaspoon pepper flakes, and 1½ tablespoons of the olive oil. Sprinkle with salt and black pepper and toss to coat the sweet potatoes evenly. Brush a large rimmed baking sheet with olive oil. Arrange the potatoes on the pan in a single layer, leaving a space in the center of the pan. Place the pan in the oven and roast the sweet potatoes for 15 minutes.

• Meanwhile, heat the remaining 1 tablespoon olive oil in a large frying pan over medium-high heat. Add the pork and brown on all sides, about 6 minutes.

• Remove the baking sheet from the oven and place the pork in the center; set the frying pan aside. Brush the pork and potatoes with some of the molasses mixture. Return the baking sheet to the oven and roast the potatoes until tender and a thermometer inserted in the thickest part of the pork registers 145°F (63°C), about 15 minutes. Transfer the pork and potatoes to a warmed platter.

• Pour off all but 1 tablespoon fat from the frying pan, and then set the frying pan over medium-high heat. Add the shallot and cook, stirring frequently and stirring up the browned bits, until it begins to soften, about 3 minutes. Add the remaining molasses mixture and the broth. Bring to a boil, stirring frequently. Simmer until the sauce thickens slightly, about 3 minutes.

• Slice the pork, and then drizzle with the sauce. Serve the pork and potatoes right away, passing any remaining sauce separately.

Toasted sesame oil, ginger, and cilantro lend an Asian twist to classic pasta with white clam sauce. The zucchini in the sauce makes this a complete entrée, so there's no need to plan a side dish. Finish with fortune cookies and sliced pears.

spaghetti with asian-flavored clams and zucchini

Spaghetti, preferably multigrain 7–8 oz (220–250 g)

Asian sesame oil, 1 tablespoon

Vegetable oil, 1 tablespoon

Fresh ginger, 1 tablespoon peeled and minced

Large shallot, 1, minced

Small zucchini, 2, cut into ⅓-inch (9-mm) cubes

Coarse kosher salt and freshly ground pepper

Clam juice or low-sodium chicken broth, ½ cup (4 fl oz/125 ml)

Rice vinegar, 1 tablespoon

Asian chile sauce, such sambal oelek or sriracha, 1 teaspoon

Manila clams, 2 lb (1 kg)

Fresh cilantro, ¼ cup (⅓ oz/10 g) minced, plus more for garnish

makes 2 servings

● Bring a large pot three-fourths full of salted water to a boil. Add the pasta, stir well, and cook until al dente, about 11 minutes. Drain, and then return to the pot. Add the sesame oil and stir to coat. Cover to keep warm.

● Meanwhile, in a heavy large frying pan over medium-high heat, warm the vegetable oil. Add the ginger and shallot and cook, stirring, until aromatic, about 30 seconds. Add the zucchini, season with salt and pepper, and sauté for 1 minute to warm. Pour in the clam juice, vinegar, and chile sauce and bring to a boil. Add the clams and the ¼ cup (⅓ oz/10 g) cilantro. Cover the pan and cook until the clams just open, about 5 minutes. Taste and adjust the seasoning.

● Transfer the pasta to individual bowls or a warmed shallow serving bowl. Pour the sauce and clams over the pasta, discarding any clams that did not open. Garnish with cilantro and serve right away.

quick tips

Tender, sweet Manila clams take only minutes to cook, and their flavorful juices become the base for a terrific sauce. If you are doubling the recipe, use a large pot to accommodate the opening shells. I enjoy this meal all year long, replacing the zucchini with other vegetables I find at the farmers' market such as asparagus, broccoli rabe, Chinese broccoli, or baby broccoli.

fall

157

Smoked turkey adds deep flavor to a simple lentil-based soup. Look for orange-fleshed sweet potatoes, sometimes labeled as yams, for their rich flavor. Greens add vivid color, nutrients, and texture. Serve with whole-grain rolls.

lentil stew with smoked turkey and sweet potatoes

fall

Olive oil, 1 tablespoon

Large onion, 1, finely chopped

Celery ribs, 3, finely chopped

Fresh thyme, 3 teaspoons minced

Low-sodium chicken broth, 8 cups (64 fl oz/2 l)

Smoked turkey leg, 1 lb (500 g), deboned, skinned, and diced, about 2 cups (¾ lb/375 g) meat

Brown lentils, 1½ cups (10½ oz/330 g), picked over and rinsed

Orange-fleshed sweet potatoes, 1¼ lb (625 g), peeled and cut into ½-inch (12-mm) cubes

Kale or chard, ½ bunch, stems removed, leaves chopped

Coarse kosher salt and freshly ground pepper

makes 6 servings

● In a heavy large saucepan over medium-high heat, warm the oil. Add the onion and celery, and sauté until almost tender, about 5 minutes. Add 2 teaspoons of the thyme and cook, stirring, until the onion is brown, about 4 minutes. Add the broth, turkey, and lentils. Cover and bring to a boil over high heat. Uncover, reduce the heat to medium-low, and simmer until the lentils are almost tender, stirring occasionally, about 30 minutes.

● Add the sweet potatoes to the pan, and simmer until almost tender, about 12 minutes. Add the kale and simmer until wilted, about 3 minutes. Season the stew to taste with salt and pepper. Mix in the remaining 1 teaspoon thyme. Ladle into warmed soup bowls and serve right away.

quick tips

The recipe makes a big pot of stew, and the flavors improve each time it is reheated. If it gets too thick, thin the stew with a little water. Smoked turkey can be replaced with smoked sausage, such as chicken or pork Andouille or kielbasa. Or, for a meatless version, leave out the turkey and use vegetable broth. Extra smoked turkey can be used as a sandwich filling, with sautéed potatoes, or as an addition to macaroni and cheese.

Italian-style sausages braised with onions, peppers, and tomatoes are a family favorite. Spoon them over creamy polenta for a hearty dinner. For a pretty look, slice the sausages before serving. Offer a romaine and olive salad on the side.

sausage and pepper ragout with polenta

Olive oil, 2 tablespoons

Hot or sweet Italian turkey or pork sausages, 1 lb (500 g)

Large red onion, 1, sliced

Large red bell peppers, 2, thinly sliced

Large poblano chile, 1, seeded and thinly sliced

Red pepper flakes, ½ teaspoon

Italian tomatoes, preferably San Marzano, 1 can (28 oz/875 g)

Dry white wine, 1 cup (8 fl oz/250 ml)

Small onion, ½, chopped

Coarse kosher salt and freshly ground black pepper

Polenta, 1 cup (7 oz/220 g)

Romano cheese, ¾ cup (3 oz/90 g) coarsely grated

Fresh marjoram, 4 tablespoons chopped

makes 4 servings

● In a large frying pan over medium-high heat, warm 1 tablespoon of the oil. Pierce the sausages several times with a small knife, add to the pan, and brown on all sides, about 8 minutes total. Transfer the sausages to a plate. Pour off all but 2 tablespoons fat from the pan. Add the red onion, bell peppers, chile, and pepper flakes, and sauté until they begin to brown, stirring up the browned bits, about 8 minutes. Add the tomatoes with their juices and the wine. Simmer for 5 minutes to blend the flavors, breaking up the tomatoes with a wooden spoon. Return the sausages to the pan, cover, and reduce the heat to low. Simmer, turning occasionally, until the sausages are cooked through, about 15 minutes.

● Meanwhile, in a heavy saucepan over medium heat, warm the remaining 1 tablespoon oil. Add the chopped onion and sauté until tender, about 5 minutes. Add 4 cups (32 fl oz/1 l) water, 1 teaspoon salt, and 1 teaspoon black pepper and bring to a boil. Gradually whisk in the polenta. Bring to a boil, stirring frequently. Reduce the heat to low and simmer slowly, stirring frequently, until the polenta is thick, about 18 minutes. Mix in the cheese and 1 tablespoon of the marjoram.

● Bring the sausage mixture to a boil. Mix in the remaining 3 tablespoons marjoram. Season to taste with salt and pepper. Spoon the polenta onto 4 warmed plates. Spoon the sausage mixture on top of the polenta, dividing it among the plates, and serve right away.

quick tips

If you are cooking for 2 people, make the entire dish. Then, spoon the leftover polenta into a pie pan and chill overnight along with the remaining ragout. When ready to serve, slice the sausages and cut the polenta into squares. Layer the polenta, sausages, and sauce in a small baking pan. Sprinkle with additional cheese and bake at 400°F (200°C) until bubbling.

One of my favorite ways to enjoy wild mushrooms is sautéed with shallots and herbs, tossed with tender pasta, and crowned with Parmesan cheese. For a superb finish, offer chunks of the cheese drizzled with aged balsamic vinegar.

fettuccine with wild mushrooms

fall

Olive oil, 1 tablespoon

Pancetta, 1½ oz (45 g), chopped

Large shallots, 3, sliced

Fresh thyme or rosemary, 2 teaspoons minced

Wild mushrooms such as chanterelles, shiitake, and/or cremini, ½–¾ lb (250–375 g), sliced

Coarse kosher salt and freshly ground pepper

Low-sodium chicken broth, ¾ cup (6 fl oz/180 ml)

Egg fettuccine, 6 oz (185 g) dried, or 9 oz (280 g) fresh

Parmesan cheese, ½ cup (2 oz/60 g) freshly grated

Fresh flat-leaf parsley, chopped, for sprinkling

makes 2 servings

● In a large frying pan over medium-high heat, warm the oil. Add the pancetta and sauté until brown, about 2 minutes. Add the shallots and thyme, and sauté until the shallots begin to brown, about 4 minutes. Add the mushrooms, sprinkle with salt and pepper, and sauté until tender, about 5 minutes. Add the broth and simmer until syrupy, about 3 minutes.

● Meanwhile, bring a large pot three-fourths full of salted water to a boil. Add the pasta, stir well, and cook until just tender, about 8 minutes for dried pasta or 4 minutes for fresh.

● Drain the pasta and add to the mushroom mixture. Stir over medium heat until coated. Mix in the cheese. Taste and adjust the seasoning. Divide the pasta between 2 warmed shallow bowls. Sprinkle with parsley and serve right away.

quick tips

Use authentic Parmigiano-Reggiano for the best flavor. This pasta is a great vehicle for chanterelle mushrooms, but more affordable shiitake or cremini mushrooms are also delicious. For best results, use fettuccine made with egg; it will be tender and silky after cooking.

I love the contrast of flavors and colors in this brightly flavored fish stew, which is enhanced with salty olives and fragrant marjoram and set against creamy polenta. End with grapes and this year's walnuts, served in their shells.

halibut with tomatoes, olives, and marjoram

Olive oil, 2 teaspoons

Onion, ½, chopped

Large shallot, 1, minced

Dry white wine, ⅔ cup
(5 fl oz/160 ml)

**Italian tomatoes,
preferably San Marzano,**
1 can (14.28 oz/448 g)

Red pepper flakes

**Coarse kosher salt and
freshly ground black pepper**

Halibut, ¾ lb (375 g), cut into
1½-inch (4-cm) pieces

Pitted kalamata olives,
¼ cup (1 oz/30 g) quartered
lengthwise

Fresh marjoram,
1–2 tablespoons chopped, or
1 teaspoon dried, crumbled

Cooked polenta or rice
for serving

makes 2 servings

● In a large frying pan over medium-high heat, warm the oil. Add the onion and shallot and sauté until tender, about 5 minutes. Add the wine and boil until reduced by half, about 4 minutes. Add the tomatoes with their juices and a pinch of pepper flakes. Sprinkle with salt and black pepper. Reduce the heat to medium and simmer until the sauce thickens slightly, breaking up the tomatoes with a wooden spoon, about 10 minutes.

● Sprinkle the fish with salt and black pepper. Add the fish to the frying pan, turn to coat it with the sauce, cover, and simmer until almost cooked through, about 4 minutes. Turn the fish pieces over, add the olives and marjoram, and simmer until the fish is cooked through, about 1 minute. Taste and adjust the seasoning.

● Spoon the polenta onto warmed plates, and then spoon the fish and sauce over the top. Serve right away.

fall

quick tips

This quick one-dish stew, which can be easily doubled for a crowd, is equally satisfying served over rice if you have it on hand in the pantry. Or, in the summer, you could replace the polenta with grilled crusty bread, which is good for soaking up the sauce. If your fishmonger does not have halibut, mahi mahi would also be good here.

This novel take on risotto is packed with caramelized onions, tender brussels sprouts, earthy shiitake mushrooms, and creamy blue cheese. It's a great way to show off autumn vegetables. Serve an endive salad to round out the meal.

fall vegetable risotto with blue cheese

Low-sodium chicken or vegetable broth, 5 cups (40 fl oz/1.25 l)

Brussels sprouts, 10 oz (315 g), ends trimmed, quartered lengthwise

Olive oil, 2 tablespoons

Large onion, 1, finely chopped

Shiitake mushrooms, ¼ lb (125 g), stems removed, sliced

Coarse kosher salt and freshly ground pepper

Arborio rice, 1½ cups (10½ oz/330 g)

Dry white wine, ½ cup (4 fl oz/125 ml)

Gorgonzola or other blue cheese, ½ cup (3 oz/90 g) crumbled

Walnut pieces, ½ cup (2 oz/60 g), toasted

makes 4 servings

● In a saucepan, bring the broth to a boil. Add the brussels sprouts and cook until bright green and almost tender, about 4 minutes. Using a slotted spoon, transfer the brussels sprouts to a bowl and set aside. Reduce the heat to low.

● In a heavy medium saucepan over medium-high heat, warm the oil. Add the onion and sauté until golden brown, about 5 minutes. Add the mushrooms, sprinkle with salt and pepper, reduce the heat to medium, and cook, stirring frequently, until they begin to soften, about 3 minutes. Add the rice and stir until opaque, about 1 minute. Add the wine and stir until absorbed. Add about ¾ cup (6 fl oz/180 ml) of the broth, and adjust the heat so the liquid bubbles and is absorbed slowly. Cook, stirring frequently, until the liquid is absorbed. Continue cooking, adding the liquid about ¾ cup at a time and stirring frequently, until the rice is just tender but slightly firm in the center and the mixture is creamy, about 20 minutes. Mix in the brussels sprouts, blue cheese, and a generous amount of pepper. Taste and adjust the seasoning.

● Spoon the risotto into warmed shallow bowls or plates, sprinkle with walnuts, and serve right away.

quick tips

Brief cooking is the key to fresh-tasting brussels sprouts. Here, they are blanched in the same broth that is used to cook the rice, which carries the flavor and nutrients of the brussels sprouts into the dish. Use vegetable broth for a meatless version, or add pancetta to make this more robust.

fall

Spicy andouille sausage and tart feta cheese add enticing flavors to this pizza topping, which shows off the last bell peppers of the season. Accompany with a romaine salad and finish with fresh seasonal fruit and amaretti cookies.

pizza with red peppers, sausage, and feta

Olive oil, 1 tablespoon, plus more as needed

Small onion, 1, finely chopped

Large red bell pepper, 1, thinly sliced, slices cut in half crosswise

Chicken or pork andouille sausages, 2 (about 6 oz total), diced

Italian tomatoes, preferably San Marzano, 1 can (14.28 ounces/488 g)

Coarse kosher salt and freshly ground pepper

Pizza dough, 1 lb (500 g) (see tips)

Cornmeal for dusting

Feta cheese, ¾ cup (3¾ oz/110 g) crumbled

Fresh basil, 2 tablespoons chopped

Fresh marjoram, 1 tablespoon chopped

makes 1 pizza; 4 servings

● In a large frying pan over medium heat, warm the 1 tablespoon oil. Add the onion and red bell pepper and sauté until they begin to soften, about 5 minutes. Add the sausage and cook until it starts to brown, about 5 minutes. Spoon off any excess fat. Add the tomatoes with their juice. Simmer, breaking up the tomatoes with a wooden spoon and stirring occasionally, until the sauce is very thick, about 10 minutes. Season the sauce to taste with salt and pepper and let cool.

● Preheat the oven to 450°F (220°C). Roll out the dough on a lightly floured work surface to an 11- to 12-inch (28- to 30-cm) round. Sprinkle a 12-inch (30-cm) pizza pan or rimless baking sheet with cornmeal; transfer the dough to the pan. Brush the dough round with oil and sprinkle with pepper. Spread the tomato sauce over the dough, leaving a ½-inch (12-mm) plain edge. Sprinkle the cheese on top of the sauce.

● Place the pizza in the oven and bake until the edges of the crust brown, about 20 minutes. Transfer the pizza to a cutting board and let stand for 5 minutes. Sprinkle with the basil and marjoram. Cut into wedges and serve.

quick tips

For ease, use purchased fresh pizza dough (avoid the dough sold in tubes) or use the recipe on page 232. For the best-tasting canned tomatoes, seek out imported San Marzano tomatoes, which are now available in many supermarkets and at specialty-food stores. Feta packed in brine keeps well, so it's easy to have it on hand to spruce up simple pizzas, pastas, and tacos.

fall

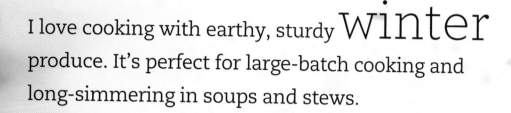

I love cooking with earthy, sturdy winter produce. It's perfect for large-batch cooking and long-simmering in soups and stews.

fresh & fast meals for **winter**

While winter produce isn't as vivid as that of the seasons that precede it, I still enjoy cooking with the root vegetables, hard-shelled squashes, and cruciferous vegetables that the season brings. This earthy produce makes perfect additions to the roasts, braises, soups, and stews that typify my seasonal cooking. In this chapter, you'll find a versatile group of roasted, simmered, sautéed and baked dishes to fulfill any craving. While satisfying, these warming, hearty dishes are also wholesome, fit into a healthy lifestyle, and are easy to do on a busy schedule.

winter market inspirations

- apples
- beets and beet greens
- belgian endive
- broccoli
- broccoli rabe
- brussels sprouts
- cabbage
- carrots
- cauliflower
- chinese broccoli
- citrus fruits
- fennel
- hard-shelled squash
- kale
- mushrooms
- parsnips
- pears
- potatoes
- radicchio
- sweet potatoes
- turnips and turnip greens

winter

add a simple side

- Toss butter lettuce with a citrus vinaigrette and top with orange or grapefruit segments and chopped fresh chives

- Sauté thinly sliced brussels sprouts in olive oil with red pepper flakes until tender, about 6 minutes; sprinkle with lemon juice

- Toss cauliflower florets in olive oil, season with salt and pepper, and roast in a 400°F (200°C) oven until tender and browned, 30 minutes

- Mash roasted sweet potatoes or hard-shelled squash and season with brown butter, chopped fresh sage, and grated Parmesan cheese

choose fruit for dessert

- Combine citrus segments with sweetened ricotta cheese in parfait glasses and dust with ground cinnamon

- Toss thin pineapple wedges with a small amount of brown sugar and broil until golden all over, about 8 minutes; splash with rum and serve with vanilla frozen yogurt

- Toss lime zest and chopped fresh mint leaves with lime juice and sugar to taste, then toss with thinly sliced Bosc pears

smart strategies for winter meals

stock up for winter I keep a quantity of dried goods and other pantry staples on hand to be sure my winter meals are varied. It's a good time to check that spices are still fresh and replace those that aren't. Great additions for winter meals are whole cloves, ancho chile powder, dried oregano, and Indian-style curry pastes. Keep a good supply of broths on hand for soups, stews, and braises.

tips for roasting Roasting is one of my favorite cooking methods for the cool-weather months. For the best results, pat dry meat, poultry, or fish with paper towels before cooking to facilitate browning. When oiling items for roasting, use only enough oil to keep the food from sticking to the pan. Finally, be sure to let meat and poultry rest for several minutes after roasting to allow their juices to re-distribute.

store sensibly Take care to let food cool slightly before refrigerating; putting too-warm foods in cold storage may warm up the refrigerator and encourage bacterial growth. Good candidates for freezing are braised meats, baked pastas, and most soups and stews; chill these items in the refrigerator before putting them in the freezer.

be flexible Being organized does not mean being rigid. In any season, be prepared to change your menus based on which ingredients at the market are freshest. You might not find the exact item you need, or you might see something that appeals to you more.

winter

173

Tangy grapefruit combined with silky avocado, red onion, and fresh cilantro makes a lively topping for wild Alaskan king salmon—one of my favorite types of sustainable fish. Serve with rice pilaf and coleslaw or sautéed cabbage.

· ·

roasted salmon with avocado and grapefruit salsa

Wild salmon fillet,
¾ lb (375 g), 1½ inches
(4 cm) thick

Olive oil

**Coarse kosher salt and
freshly ground pepper**

Ancho chile powder

Large grapefruit, 1

Small, firm but ripe avocado,
1, pitted, peeled, and cubed

Large jalapeño chile,
½, seeded and minced

Red onion, 3 tablespoons
minced

Fresh cilantro,
2 tablespoons minced

Fresh lime juice,
1 tablespoon

makes 2 servings

● Preheat the oven to 375°F (190°C). In a small baking pan, place the fish. Brush on both sides with olive oil. Sprinkle with salt, pepper, and ancho chile powder. Place in the oven and roast until almost opaque in the center, about 18 minutes.

● Meanwhile, using a sharp knife, cut off the peel and all of the white pith from all around the grapefruit. Working over a small bowl, use the knife to cut between the membranes to release the grapefruit segments into the bowl. Squeeze the juice from the membranes into the bowl. Remove the grapefruit segments from the bowl and cut crosswise into ½-inch (12-mm) pieces; return to the bowl. Gently mix in the avocado, jalapeño, onion, cilantro, and lime juice. Season the salsa to taste with salt and pepper.

● Cut the fish in half and divide between 2 warmed plates. Spoon the salsa over the top and serve right away.

· ·

quick tips

Ancho chile powder, found in the spice section in supermarkets, provides the rich flavor of anchos without having to roast the chiles. It can also be used on chicken, shrimp, and other fish. This recipe can be doubled for a family of four, or tripled for a dinner party for six.

Chicken, onions, and herbs braised with wine make a warming meal for a cold evening. Serve the chicken over polenta or rice, or set out some crusty bread, to absorb the flavorful juices. Sautéed greens make a colorful accompaniment.

braised chicken with onions, rosemary, and sage

Large chicken breast halves and thighs, 3½ lb (1.75 kg), breasts cut in half crosswise

Coarse kosher salt and freshly ground pepper

Olive oil, 3 tablespoons

Large onions, 2, 1 finely chopped and 1 cut into 1-inch (2.5-cm) pieces

Pancetta, 2 oz (60 g), chopped

Fresh rosemary, 2 teaspoons minced

Fresh sage, 1½ teaspoons minced

Small bay leaves, 3

Whole cloves, 4

Tomato paste, 1½ tablespoons

Dry white wine, 1 cup (8 fl oz/250 ml)

Low-sodium chicken broth, 2 cups (16 fl oz/500 ml)

makes 4 servings

Pat the chicken pieces dry with paper towels, and sprinkle on both sides with salt and pepper. In a heavy large, deep frying pan over medium-high heat, warm 2 tablespoons of the oil. Add the chicken pieces and cook until brown on both sides. Transfer the chicken to a plate.

Pour off the fat from the frying pan. Add the remaining 1 tablespoon oil to the pan. Add the chopped onion, onion pieces, pancetta, rosemary, sage, bay leaves, and cloves. Sauté until the onions begin to brown, about 8 minutes. Stir in the tomato paste. Add the wine and bring to a boil, stirring up the browned bits.

Return the chicken to the frying pan with any juices accumulated on the plate. Add the broth and bring to a boil. Reduce the heat to medium-low and simmer until the chicken breast pieces are cooked through, frequently spooning the cooking liquid over, and turning, about 20 minutes. Transfer the chicken breast pieces to a plate. Continue cooking the thighs until tender, about 15 minutes longer. Return the breasts to the frying pan and simmer until heated through, about 3 minutes. Taste and adjust the seasoning. Serve right away.

quick tips

I discovered organic farmed chickens at my supermarket a couple of years ago, and love the pure, clean flavor they offer. To me, the extra cost for organic products is worth it. For even fuller flavor, season the chicken 30 minutes before cooking. When stocking your pantry, look for tomato paste in a tube instead of in a can; it keeps for ages in the refrigerator.

winter

On my quest to eat more greens, I bought broccoli rabe at the farmers' market and was delighted by how sweet it tastes in contrast to the warming heat of chile sauce in this meatless dish. Serve over brown jasmine or basmati rice.

stir-fried tofu with mushrooms and greens

Low-sodium vegetable or chicken broth, 1 cup (8 fl oz/250 ml)

Low-sodium soy sauce, 2 tablespoons

Cornstarch, 1 tablespoon

Red wine vinegar, 1 tablespoon

Asian sesame oil, 1 tablespoon

Freshly ground pepper, ¾ teaspoon

Asian chile sauce such as sambal oelek, ½ teaspoon

Sugar, ½ teaspoon

Vegetable oil, 1 tablespoon

Green onions, ¼ cup (1 oz/30 g) minced

Fresh ginger, 2 tablespoons peeled and minced

Fresh shiitake mushrooms, ¼ lb (125 g), stemmed and sliced

Broccoli rabe, 1 large bunch, cut into 1½-inch (4-cm) lengths

Firm tofu, about 1 lb (500 g), drained, patted dry, and cut into ¾-inch (2-cm) cubes

Coarse kosher salt

makes 4 servings

● In a small bowl, combine the broth, soy sauce, cornstarch, vinegar, sesame oil, pepper, chile sauce, and sugar.

● In a small wok or large nonstick frying pan over medium-high heat, warm the oil. Add the green onions and ginger and toss and stir until aromatic, about 30 seconds. Add the mushrooms and stir until coated with oil, about 30 seconds. Add the broccoli rabe and stir until heated through, about 1 minute.

● Cover the pan and cook, stirring occasionally, until the broccoli rabe is just tender-crisp, about 3 minutes. Uncover, add the tofu, and stir gently. Stir the broth mixture to dissolve the cornstarch, and then add to the frying pan. Cook until the sauce thickens and the tofu is heated through, 2–3 minutes. Season to taste with salt and serve right away.

quick tips

Put rice on to cook just before starting to prepare this dish; both will be ready at about the same time. Sambal oelek—one of my favorite pantry staples for quick cooking—can be found in the Asian section of most markets. If you like garlic, you can use chile-garlic sauce instead. If you can find Chinese broccoli, it works just as well as broccoli rabe.

winter

Pleasantly bitter broccoli rabe, lightly sharp feta cheese, and refreshing mint perk up tomato sauce in an inventive meatless meal. I use sheep's milk cheese for its fresh, authentic flavor. The pasta is so satisfying, no side dish is needed.

broccoli rabe, feta, and mint **pasta**

Olive oil, 1 tablespoon

Pancetta, 2 oz (60 g) chopped (optional)

Onion, 1, finely chopped

Red pepper flakes

Italian tomatoes, preferably San Marzano, 1 can (28 oz/875 g)

Coarse kosher salt and freshly ground pepper

Broccoli rabe, 2 bunches (about 1¾ lb/875 g total weight), cut into 1-inch (2.5-cm) pieces

Rotini pasta, preferably multigrain, 14½–16 oz (410–500 g)

Fresh mint, ¼ cup chopped

Feta cheese, ¾ cup (¼ lb/125 g) crumbled

makes 4 servings

● In a large frying pan over medium heat, warm the oil. Add the pancetta, if using, and sauté until brown, about 5 minutes. Add the onion and 2 large pinches of red pepper flakes to the pan and sauté until the onion is tender, about 8 minutes. Add the tomatoes and 1 cup (8 fl oz/250 ml) water and bring to a boil, breaking up the tomatoes with a spoon. Reduce the heat to medium-low and simmer until the sauce thickens and the flavors blend, 15–20 minutes. Taste and adjust the seasoning with salt and pepper.

● Meanwhile, bring a large pot three-fourths full of salted water to a boil. Add the broccoli rabe and cook until just tender-crisp, about 4 minutes. Using a slotted spoon, transfer the broccoli rabe to a bowl. Add the pasta to the pot, stir well, and cook until al dente, about 11 minutes. Return the broccoli rabe to the pot and cook until heated through, about 30 seconds.

● Drain the pasta and broccoli rabe. Return to the same pot. Add the sauce and mint and stir to coat. Mix in ½ cup (3 oz/90 g) of the cheese. Taste and adjust the seasoning. Transfer the pasta to a warmed shallow bowl. Sprinkle with the remaining cheese and serve right away.

quick tips

Keep pancetta, high-quality canned tomatoes, red pepper flakes, and pasta on hand in the pantry for quick dinners that need no advance planning. Crumbled fresh goat cheese or grated pecorino romano cheese are delicious alternatives to the feta. Feel free to substitute any short pasta shapes such as fusilli or penne for the rotini.

winter

Alaskan halibut is sustainable and delicious. Here, I use a quick homemade spice blend to season both the fish and vegetables. Offer couscous, or basmati or jasmine rice, on the side. Chopped fresh cilantro makes a refreshing garnish.

spiced **roasted halibut** with fennel and onion

Ground cumin, 1½ teaspoons

Chili powder, 1½ teaspoons

Ground cinnamon, 1 teaspoon

Ground turmeric, ¼ teaspoon

Large fennel bulb, 1, cut lengthwise into 1-inch (2.5-cm) wedges

Large red onion, 1, halved lengthwise, then cut lengthwise through the root end into ½-inch (12-mm) wedges

Olive oil, 3 tablespoons

Coarse kosher salt and freshly ground pepper

Halibut fillets, 2 (about 6 oz/185 g each)

Chopped fresh cilantro

makes 2 servings; can be doubled

● Preheat the oven to 450°F (230°C). In a small bowl, combine the cumin, chili powder, cinnamon, and turmeric. Combine the fennel and onion wedges in a 10-by-14-inch (25-by-35-cm) metal baking pan. Add 2 tablespoons of the oil to the vegetables and toss to coat. Sprinkle with 1 tablespoon of the spice mixture and toss. Sprinkle with salt and pepper. Spread the vegetables in a single layer. Roast the vegetables until tender and browned, turning once, about 35 minutes.

● Meanwhile, brush a small baking pan with oil. Brush the fish fillets with oil on both sides, sprinkle lightly on both sides with the spice mixture, and salt and pepper. Roast until the fish is almost firm to the touch, 5–8 minutes, depending on the thickness of the fillet.

● Transfer the fish and vegetables to warmed plates, garnish with cilantro, and serve right away.

quick tips

Halibut dries out easily, so be careful to not overcook the fish; it is better to err on the rare side. Mix up an extra portion of the spice blend to use on roasted or grilled shrimp, chicken, or salmon.

winter

Bread crumbs mixed with fragrant lemon zest, crunchy walnuts, spicy mustard, and aromatic shallot form a crispy crust on chicken breasts and seal in the natural juices. Serve with steamed broccoli or wilted winter greens and rice.

chicken with mustard and walnut coating

Skinless, boneless chicken breast halves, 4 (about 5 oz/155 g each)

Large egg, 1

Dijon mustard, 2 tablespoons

Panko (Japanese bread crumbs), ½ cup (½ oz/15 g)

Walnuts, ¼ cup (1 oz/30 g) finely chopped

Small shallot, 1, minced

Grated lemon zest, 1½ teaspoons

Dry mustard, ½ teaspoon

Cayenne pepper, ⅛ teaspoon

Olive oil, 2 tablespoons

Coarse kosher salt and freshly ground pepper

makes 4 servings

● Position a rack in the lower third of the oven and preheat to 400°F (200°C).

● Place the chicken breast halves between 2 sheets of waxed paper; using a meat mallet or rolling pin, pound the breasts to a thickness of ⅓–½ inch (9–12 mm). In a shallow bowl, combine the egg and Dijon mustard; whisk to blend well. In a pie pan, combine the panko, walnuts, shallot, lemon zest, dry mustard, and cayenne; mix to blend well. In a large ovenproof nonstick frying pan over medium heat, warm the oil. Place the chicken breasts in the egg-mustard mixture and turn to coat. Season with salt and pepper. Dip the chicken in the panko, turning to coat.

● Add the chicken to the pan and cook until golden brown on the first side, about 2 minutes. Turn the chicken over, and then place the frying pan in the oven. Bake the chicken until springy to the touch, about 8 minutes.

● Transfer the chicken to warmed plates and serve right away.

quick tips

The chicken is quickly browned in a frying pan, and then finishes cooking in the same pan in the oven, making for easy cleanup. Prepare the vegetables while the chicken bakes. Panko, Japanese bread crumbs, adds great texture with no work; keep a package in the pantry for ease.

Smoked paprika and cumin add memorable flavors to this hearty winter soup, and sausage lends both flavor and substance. I like to serve it with slices of seeded baguette and finish the meal with fresh tangerines and crisp cookies.

smoky **black bean soup**

Olive oil, 1 tablespoon

Red bell peppers, 4, diced

Celery ribs, 3, finely diced

Onion, 1, finely chopped

Fully cooked smoked turkey, chicken, or pork sausage, 1–2, chopped

Ground cumin, 1 teaspoon

Smoked hot paprika, 1 teaspoon

Low-sodium chicken broth, 4 cups (32 fl oz/1 l)

Black beans, 2 cans (15 oz/470 g each), rinsed and drained

Diced tomatoes with juice, 1 can (14.5 oz/455 g)

Water or low-sodium chicken broth, 2 cups (16 fl oz/500 ml), or as needed

Coarse kosher salt and freshly ground pepper

makes 4–6 servings

● In a heavy medium pot over medium-high heat, warm the oil. Add the peppers, celery, and onion, and sauté until the onion is tender, 5–6 minutes. Add the sausage and sauté until browned, about 2 minutes. Add the cumin and paprika, and stir for 1 minute. Add the broth, beans, and tomatoes. Bring the soup to a boil, reduce the heat, and simmer to blend the flavors, at least 20 minutes and up to 45 minutes, thinning with water or more broth as desired.

● Season the soup to taste with salt and pepper. Ladle the soup into warmed bowls and serve right away.

quick tips

This soup is fine after 20 minutes of simmering, but it's even better after 45 minutes or reheated on the next night. If the soup gets too thick, thin it to the desired consistency with more broth or water. This basic recipe is easily varied: Replace the black beans with white beans or chickpeas; choose Andouille or kielbasa sausage; or select parsnips, sweet potatoes, or cabbage in place of the peppers.

Sweet, tart applesauce balanced with spicy horseradish is an unusually good accent for seared pork chops. Sautéed shaved brussels sprouts add good color and nutrients to the plate. Sliced pears and cheese are the perfect finale.

pork chops with horseradish applesauce

Center-cut loin pork chops, 2, each 1¼–1½ inch (3–4 cm) thick

Coarse kosher salt and freshly ground pepper

Fresh rosemary, 2 teaspoons minced

Fresh sage, 2 teaspoons minced

Unsweetened applesauce, 1 cup (9 oz/280 g)

Cream-style horseradish, 2 teaspoons

Sugar, 4 teaspoons

Olive oil, 1 tablespoon

Shallot, 1, minced

Dry vermouth or dry white wine, ½ cup (4 fl oz/125 ml)

Low-sodium chicken broth, ½ cup (4 fl oz/125 ml)

makes 2 servings; can be doubled

- Sprinkle the pork chops on both sides with salt and pepper, and then with 1½ teaspoons each of the rosemary and sage. In a small bowl, combine the applesauce, horseradish, and sugar, and stir to blend.

- In a heavy medium frying pan over high heat, warm the oil. Add the pork and cook until lightly browned, 1–2 minutes per side. Reduce the heat to medium-low, cover, and cook until the meat feels firm but not hard when pressed and an instant-read thermometer registers 145°F (63°C), 3–4 minutes per side. Transfer the pork to a warmed plate and cover with foil.

- Pour off all but 1 tablespoon fat from the frying pan. Set the pan over medium heat, add the shallot, and sauté until fragrant, about 30 seconds. Add the vermouth, broth, and remaining ½ teaspoon each rosemary and sage. Boil until syrupy, stirring up the browned bits on the pan bottom, about 2 minutes.

- Return the chops to the frying pan, and turn a few times to absorb the flavors. Transfer the pork to warmed plates; spoon the sauce over the top. Serve right away with the applesauce.

quick tips

For succulent pork chops, make certain they sizzle both while browning and after they are covered, adjusting the heat as needed. Don't overcook the pork, or it will be dry; I always test it with an instant-read thermometer to be sure. A quick sauce made in the pan in which the pork was cooked takes advantage of the delicious pan drippings—you don't want to waste them.

Fennel and mustard seeds add flavor and texture to the mild fish, which is topped off with an easy and refreshing shallot-parsley-lemon garnish. Rice or mashed potatoes and a fennel and orange salad are perfect accompaniments.

tuna with shallot gremolata

Albacore tuna steak,
1½ lb (750 g), about 1 inch (2.5 cm) thick

Mustard seeds, 1 teaspoon

Fennel seeds, 1 teaspoon

Coarse kosher salt and freshly ground pepper

Lemon, 1

Fresh flat-leaf parsley,
⅓ cup (½ oz/15 g) chopped

Shallot, 1, minced

Olive oil, 1 teaspoon

makes 4 servings

● Cut the tuna into 4 pieces and place in a shallow baking pan. Press the mustard seeds and fennel seeds into both sides of the tuna. Sprinkle both sides with salt and pepper. Set aside while making the gremolata.

● To make the gremolata, finely grate the zest from the lemon and place the zest in a small bowl (reserve the lemon for another use). Add the parsley and shallot to the bowl and mix well.

● In a large nonstick frying pan over medium-high heat, warm the oil. Add the fish and cook as desired, 2–3 minutes per side for medium-rare. Arrange the fish on a warmed serving platter or divide among 4 warmed plates. Sprinkle with the gremolata and serve right away.

quick tips

Sourcing tuna that is fished in a responsible way and that is low in mercury can be tricky. Albacore and yellow fin (also called ahi) are usually good choices. For more information on sustainable seafood, check the Monterey Bay Aquarium's Seafood Watch website (see page 229). The gremolata is delicious on roasted chicken breasts or any fish; it can also be used to perk up a long-simmered stew.

winter

Braising is a favorite way to cook chicken; the ingredients mingle, forming something more delicious than the sum of their parts. Here, squash, turnips, and mushrooms add deep flavor to chicken thighs. Serve with rice or bread.

chicken with squash, turnips, and shiitakes

Olive oil, 2 tablespoons

Skinless, boneless chicken thighs, 1¼ lb (625 g)

Coarse kosher salt and freshly ground pepper

Large onion, 1, finely chopped

Fresh sage, 1 tablespoon minced

Butternut squash, 1 lb (500 g), peeled, seeded, and cut into ½-inch (12-mm) pieces

Small turnips, 2 bunches, unpeeled, cut into ½-inch (12-mm) pieces, greens reserved

Low-sodium chicken broth, 1½ cups (12 fl oz/375 ml), plus 1 tablespoon

Shiitake mushrooms, ½ lb (250 g), stemmed, and cut into 1-inch (2.5-cm) pieces

All-purpose flour, 1¼ teaspoons

makes 4 servings

● In a heavy large frying pan over medium-high heat, warm 1 tablespoon of the oil. Sprinkle the chicken with salt and pepper. Add the chicken to the frying pan and brown, about 1½ minutes per side. Using tongs, transfer the chicken to a plate. Reduce the heat to medium; add the onion and sage, and sauté until tender, about 5 minutes. Add the squash and turnips, and stir to coat with oil. Add 1½ cups (12 fl oz/375 ml) of the broth. Bring to a boil, reduce the heat to medium-low, cover, and simmer until the chicken is tender, about 25 minutes.

● Meanwhile, in a large nonstick frying pan over medium-high heat, warm the remaining 1 tablespoon oil. Add the mushrooms, sprinkle with salt and pepper, and sauté until tender, about 3 minutes. Remove from the heat. Chop the greens from 1 bunch of the turnips (reserve the remainder for another use).

● Add the mushrooms and chopped turnip greens to the chicken. Cover and simmer until the greens wilt, about 5 minutes. In a small bowl, place the flour; gradually add the remaining 1 tablespoon chicken broth, mixing until smooth. Add to the frying pan, mix it in, cover, and simmer until the sauce thickens, about 2 minutes. Taste and adjust the seasoning and serve right away.

quick tips

For ease of preparation, purchase peeled and cubed squash from the market. I like to add some of the turnip greens for color, nutrition, and good flavor, but they can also be omitted, if you wish. Reheat the leftovers for an even richer flavor than on the first night.

Rich Italian sausage, earthy button mushrooms, and salty-nutty Parmesan cheese flavor this robust risotto, perfect for a cold winter night by the fire. Serve with a romaine and fennel salad tossed with olive oil and balsamic vinegar.

sausage and mushroom **risotto**

Low-sodium chicken broth, 5 cups (40 fl oz/1.25 l)

Olive oil, 1 tablespoon

Onion, 1, finely chopped

Italian sausage, ¾ lb (375 g), casings removed

Button mushrooms, 10–12 oz (315–375 g), sliced

Arborio rice, 1½ cups (10½ oz/330 g)

Dry vermouth or dry white wine, ½ cup (4 fl oz/125 ml)

Coarse kosher salt and freshly ground pepper

Grated Parmesan or Romano cheese, ½ cup (2 oz/60 g), plus more as needed

Fresh flat-leaf parsley or basil, minced, for garnish

makes 4 servings

• In a saucepan, bring the broth to a boil. Reduce the heat to low and keep the broth warm while you are making the risotto.

• In a heavy saucepan over medium-high heat, warm the oil. Add the chopped onion and cook, stirring frequently, until almost tender, about 5 minutes. Add the sausage and cook, breaking up the meat with a spoon, until it is no longer pink, about 4 minutes. Add the mushrooms and sauté until they begin to soften, about 5 minutes. Add the rice and stir until it is opaque, about 1 minute. Add the vermouth and stir until absorbed, about 2 minutes.

• Add about ¾ cup (6 fl oz/180 ml) of the broth to the pan and adjust the heat so the liquid bubbles and is absorbed slowly. Cook, stirring frequently, until the liquid is absorbed. Continue to cook, adding the broth about ¾ cup at a time, and stirring frequently until the rice is just tender but slightly firm in the center and the mixture is creamy, about 20 minutes.

• Mix in the ½ cup (2 oz/60 g) Parmesan cheese. Season the risotto to taste with salt and pepper. Spoon the risotto into warmed bowls. Sprinkle with minced parsley and serve right away.

quick tips

This dish works well with either hot or sweet pork or turkey Italian sausage. If you are cooking for two, make the entire recipe, and then turn leftovers into risotto cakes: mix an egg yolk and ½ cup (½ oz/15 g) panko (Japanese bread crumbs) into the cold risotto. Form the mixture into cakes ¾ inch (2 cm) thick, coat with egg and more panko, and then brown in olive oil.

This is my favorite comforting dinner after a rough day. To save time, I use a vibrant prepared curry paste to flavor the mild ingredients. Spoon it over rice and serve purchased chutney alongside. Choose a fruit sorbet for dessert.

cauliflower and tofu **curry**

Olive oil, 1 tablespoon

Large onion, 1, finely chopped

Firm tofu, 14–16 oz (440–500 g) drained, patted dry, and cut into ¾-inch (2-cm) cubes

Hot curry or vindaloo curry paste, preferably Patak, 1 heaping tablespoon

Diced tomatoes, 1 can (14.5 oz/455 g)

Cauliflower, 1 head, cut into ¾-inch (2-cm) florets

Cooked brown basmati or brown jasmine rice

makes 4 servings

● In a large frying pan over medium-high heat, warm the oil. Add the onion and sauté until almost tender, about 5 minutes. Add the tofu and sauté until warm, about 2 minutes. Add the curry paste and stir to coat the tofu well. Add the tomatoes and their juice, the cauliflower, and 1½ cups (12 fl oz/375 ml) water. Bring the mixture to a boil, cover, reduce the heat to medium-low, and simmer until the cauliflower is tender and the sauce thickens slightly, about 20 minutes. Add more water if the sauce gets too thick.

● Spoon the rice into warmed shallow bowls. Spoon the tofu-cauliflower mixture over the top and serve right away.

quick tips

High-quality curry pastes add tons of good flavor to tofu, chicken, or fish; I always have a few jars in the cupboard. My favorite pastes, made by Patak, are the spicy Hot Curry, equally spicy Vindaloo, and aromatic Garam Masala. If you prefer milder food, try the Mild Curry paste. This dish reheats well, and I always look forward to the even easier dinner on the next night.

winter

Chicken thighs become succulent and tender when braised with white wine and hearty winter herbs; down-to-earth parsnips and carrots add sweetness to the mix. Spooned over egg noodles, this makes a comforting one-dish winter meal.

chicken and noodles with sweet root vegetables

Large chicken thighs,
4 (about 1½ lb/750 g)

Coarse kosher salt and freshly ground pepper

All-purpose flour
for dredging

Extra-virgin olive oil,
2 tablespoons

Large red onion, 1, chopped

Parsnips, ½ lb (250 g), peeled, halved lengthwise, and cut on the diagonal into ½-inch (12-mm) pieces

Carrots, ½ lb (250 g), peeled, halved lengthwise, and cut on the diagonal into ½-inch (12-mm) pieces

Fresh sage or rosemary,
1 tablespoon minced

Dry white wine, ½ cup
(4 fl oz/125 ml)

Low-sodium chicken broth,
1¼ cups (10 fl oz/310 ml)

Wide egg noodles, 6 oz
(185 g)

Fresh flat-leaf parsley,
minced (optional)

makes 4 servings

• Remove the skin from the chicken, if desired, and cut away any excess fat. Sprinkle the chicken with salt and pepper. Dredge the chicken in flour to coat on all sides. In a large nonstick frying pan over medium-high heat, warm 1 tablespoon of the oil. Add the chicken and cook until light brown, about 4 minutes per side. Transfer to a plate. Add the onion, parsnips, carrots, and sage to the frying pan; sprinkle with salt and pepper. Sauté until the onion is tender, stirring frequently, about 10 minutes.

• Add the wine and boil until reduced by about half, stirring up the browned bits on the pan bottom, about 2 minutes. Return the chicken to the pan. Add the broth and bring to a boil. Reduce the heat to low, cover, and simmer, turning after 10 minutes, until the chicken is tender, about 20 minutes. Uncover and simmer until the liquid thickens slightly, about 5 minutes. Taste and adjust the seasoning.

• Meanwhile, bring a large pot three-fourths full of salted water to a boil. Add the noodles, stir well, and cook until just tender, about 7 minutes.

• Drain the noodles and transfer to a warmed shallow bowl. Add the remaining 1 tablespoon oil and toss to coat well. Divide the noodles among 4 warmed plates and spoon the chicken mixture over the top. Sprinkle servings with parsley, if desired, and serve right away.

quick tips

Chicken thighs stay juicy when reheated; if you are cooking for two, make the entire recipe and save the rest for a meal on another night. Instead of dry white wine, try an off-dry Gewürztraminer for the stew and then, if you like, pour the rest of the wine with the meal.

winter

A bold mustard and caper sauce and colorful radicchio salad make a simple burger extra-special. I like to serve the patties on grilled buns, which have a great texture. Offer fresh carrot sticks and chips on the side.

turkey burgers with radicchio slaw

Mayonnaise, 3 tablespoons

Whole-grain Dijon mustard, 1½ tablespoons

Capers, 3 tablespoons, rinsed and minced

Ground turkey, preferably dark meat, 1¼ lb (625 g)

Fresh thyme, 1 tablespoon minced

Extra-virgin olive oil, 4 tablespoons (2 fl oz/60 ml), plus more as needed

Large shallot, 1, minced

Coarse kosher salt and freshly ground pepper

Hamburger buns, preferably potato buns, 4

Radicchio, 1 head, cut into quarters, then thinly sliced

Balsamic vinegar, 1½ tablespoons

makes 4 servings

In a small bowl, combine the mayonnaise, mustard, and 1½ tablespoons of the capers. Set the sauce aside.

In a medium bowl, combine the turkey, thyme, and remaining 1½ tablespoons of the capers. In a small frying pan over medium heat, warm 1 tablespoon of the oil. Add the shallot and sauté until tender, about 4 minutes. Add to the turkey. Add ¾ teaspoon salt and a generous amount of pepper. Mix gently to combine. Form the mixture into 4 patties, each about ½ inch (12 mm) thick. Brush the cut surface of the buns with olive oil, and sprinkle with pepper.

Preheat the broiler. Heat a large frying pan over medium heat; brush with oil. Add the patties and cook until cooked through, about 5 minutes on each side.

Meanwhile, in another bowl, place the sliced radicchio. Add the remaining 3 tablespoons oil and toss to coat. Sprinkle lightly with salt and pepper, add the vinegar, and toss to coat. Taste the slaw and adjust the seasoning.

Place the hamburger buns, cut side up, on a rimmed baking sheet. Place under the broiler and broil, watching carefully, until golden brown, about 4 minutes.

Divide bun bottoms among 4 warmed plates. Top each with a patty, spoon some sauce and then radicchio slaw over each patty, and top with bun tops. Spoon the remaining slaw alongside the burgers and serve right away.

quick tips

Make extra sauce to use as a dip for fresh vegetables or to serve with fish. Any type of turkey meat works well here: dark, white, or a mixture; ground chicken is also delicious in these burgers. The patties and sauce can be made 1 day ahead and refrigerated.

winter

Caramelized onions, rosemary-scented wild mushrooms, and creamy Brie are a matchless combination for this meatless pizza—no tomato sauce is needed here. Serve with a colorful red leaf lettuce salad dressed with balsamic vinaigrette.

pizza with onions, mushrooms, and brie

Olive oil, 3 tablespoons, plus more as needed

Large onions, 2, halved and thinly sliced

Fresh rosemary, 1 tablespoon minced

Coarse kosher salt and freshly ground pepper

Dry white wine, ¼ cup (2 fl oz/60 ml)

Chanterelle, shiitake, or cremini mushrooms, ½ lb (250 g), sliced

Large shallot, 1, minced

Fresh flat-leaf parsley, 1 tablespoon minced, plus more for garnish

Cornmeal for dusting

Pizza dough, 1 lb (500 g) (see tips)

Brie cheese, ½ lb (250 g), rind trimmed, cut into small pieces

makes 1 pizza; 4 servings

● Preheat the oven to 425°F (220°C). In a large nonstick frying pan over medium heat, warm 1½ tablespoons of the oil. Add the onions and rosemary. Sprinkle with salt and pepper, and sauté until golden, about 20 minutes. Add the wine and simmer until evaporated, about 1 minute. Transfer the onions to a bowl. Wipe out the frying pan, set over medium-high heat, and warm the remaining 1½ tablespoons oil. Add the mushrooms and shallot. Season with salt and pepper. Sauté until the mushrooms are tender and juices evaporate, about 5 minutes. Remove from the heat. Mix in 1 tablespoon parsley.

● Brush a large baking sheet with oil and sprinkle with cornmeal. On a lightly floured surface, roll out the dough to a round 10–11 inches (25–28 cm) in diameter. Transfer the crust to the baking sheet. Brush the crust with oil. Spread the onions and then the mushrooms over the crust, leaving a border. Sprinkle with the cheese. Bake until the crust browns and the cheese melts, 12–15 minutes.

● Transfer the pizza to a cutting board. Cut into wedges. Sprinkle with parsley and serve right away.

quick tips

Any mushroom tastes great on this pizza—shiitake, crimini, or button are all good choices in winter. This pizza is also a delicious way to showcase fall's fleeting chanterelles. If you want to add a little meat, sauté Italian sausage or pancetta along with the mushrooms. Use a quality purchased pizza dough or follow the recipe on page 232.

Chopped shallots, fresh thyme, orange zest, and fennel seeds do triple work here, flavoring the lamb, vegetables, and sauce. Roast halved fingerling potatoes, tossed with olive oil and rosemary, in a hot oven to serve alongside the lamb.

broiled leg of lamb with orange and fennel

Shallot, 2 tablespoons minced

Fresh thyme, 2 tablespoons minced

Grated orange zest, 2 tablespoons

Fennel seeds, 2¼ teaspoons, crushed

Boneless leg of lamb, 1¼–1½ lb (625–750 g), fat well trimmed

Coarse kosher salt and freshly ground pepper

Olive oil, 1 tablespoon, plus more for brushing

Large fennel bulb, 1, cut lengthwise into wedges ¼–½ inch (6–12 mm) thick

Large red onion, 1, cut lengthwise into wedges ¼–½ inch (6–12 mm) thick

Dry vermouth, ⅓ cup (3 fl oz/80 ml)

Low-sodium chicken broth, ⅓ cup (3 fl oz/80 ml)

makes 4 servings

● In a small bowl, mix the shallot, thyme, orange zest, and fennel seeds. Place the lamb on a broiler pan and sprinkle both sides with salt and a generous amount of pepper. Rub 1 tablespoon of the shallot mixture into each side of the lamb. Brush all over with olive oil. In a large bowl, combine the fennel bulb and onion; add 1 tablespoon oil and toss to coat. Set aside 1 tablespoon of the shallot mixture for the sauce; add the remaining shallot mixture to the vegetables and toss to coat. Sprinkle with salt and pepper. Brush a heavy large baking sheet with with olive oil; transfer the vegetables to the sheet and arrange in a single layer.

● Position an oven rack so the meat will be 4 inches (10 cm) from the heat source, and preheat the broiler. Broil the lamb until a thermometer inserted in the thickest part registers 125°–130°F (52°–54°C) for medium-rare, about 8 minutes per side. Transfer the lamb to a warmed platter and tent loosely with foil.

● Adjust the oven rack so the vegetables will be 2–3 inches (5–7.5 cm) from the heat source. Broil the vegetables until they start to brown, 3–4 minutes per side.

● Degrease the juices in the bottom part of the broiler pan. Set the pan on the stove top over medium heat. Add the vermouth and bring to a boil, stirring up the browned bits. Boil until syrupy, about 3 minutes. Add the broth and boil until it thickens slightly, about 2 minutes. Mix in the reserved shallot mixture and any lamb juices from the platter. Taste and adjust the seasoning.

● Slice the meat thinly and serve right away with the vegetables and sauce.

quick tips

Leftovers make terrific sandwiches for lunch or a superquick dinner. The seasoning mixture can be made one day ahead and sprinkled on the lamb; that way the meat is ready to cook when you get home from a busy day.

winter

I like the simplicity of this dish: thin chicken cutlets are quickly sautéed, and then a quick pan sauce is created by cooking together fresh herbs, tart lemon juice, and hot chiles. Serve with mashed potatoes and sautéed savoy cabbage.

chicken sauté with thyme, lemon, and chile

Olive oil, 2 tablespoons

Chicken breast cutlets,
(¾ lb/375 g)

Coarse kosher salt and freshly ground pepper

Large shallot, 1, minced

Fresh thyme, 2 teaspoons minced

Serrano chile, ½–1, minced

Dry white wine, ⅓ cup
(3 fl oz/80 ml)

Fresh lemon juice,
2 tablespoons

makes 2 servings

● In a large frying pan over medium-high heat, warm 1 tablespoon of the oil. Sprinkle the chicken with salt and pepper and add to the frying pan. Sauté until cooked through, 2–3 minutes per side. Transfer the chicken to 2 warmed plates.

● Add the remaining 1 tablespoon oil to the same frying pan, and then add the shallot, thyme, and chile. Sauté until the shallot begins to soften, about 1 minute. Add the wine and lemon juice, and boil, stirring up the browned bits on the pan bottom, until syrupy, about 1 minute. Remove the pan from the heat. Add any juices from the plate holding the chicken to the sauce and stir well. Taste and adjust the seasoning. Spoon the sauce over the chicken and serve right away.

quick tips

Chicken breast cutlets are a great resource for cooks who have little time on their hands. I buy organic chicken for the best flavor. The recipe can be easily doubled, so make a big batch. The next day, cut up the leftovers, heat the chicken in the remaining sauce, then spoon over hot cooked rice or noodles.

winter

Here, seasonings are blended in a food processor to make an easy Asian-style curry paste. I use yogurt and just a touch of coconut milk to create a hybrid of Thai and Indian flavors. Serve over brown rice to enjoy the enticing sauce.

curried mahi mahi with chinese broccoli

Onion, ⅓ cup (1½ oz/45 g) chopped

Large shallots, 3, halved

Fresh cilantro, 2 tablespoons chopped stems, plus chopped leaves for garnish

Fresh lemongrass, 2 tablespoons chopped from bottom 6 inches (15 cm) of the stalk

Fresh ginger, 2 tablespoons peeled and chopped

Turmeric, 1 tablespoon

Ground cumin, 1 tablespoon

Red pepper flakes, ¾ teaspoon

Vegetable oil, 1 tablespoon

Mahi mahi, 1½ lb (750 g), cut into 2-inch (5-cm) pieces

Plain yogurt, 1½ cups (12 oz/375 g)

Clam juice, 1½ cups (12 fl oz/375 ml)

Coconut milk or heavy cream, 2 tablespoons (optional)

Chinese broccoli or broccoli rabe, 2 bunches, cut into 2-inch (5-cm) pieces

makes 4 servings

In a food processor, combine the onion, shallots, cilantro stems, lemongrass, ginger, turmeric, cumin, and pepper flakes. Process until finely ground, stopping frequently to scrape down the sides of the work bowl.

In a large nonstick frying pan over medium-high heat, warm the oil. Add the curry paste and stir for 1 minute. Add the mahi mahi and cook, turning occasionally, for 2 minutes. Whisk the yogurt until smooth and add it to the pan, then stir in the clam juice and coconut milk, if using. Simmer, turning occasionally, until the fish is almost cooked through, about 6 minutes. Transfer the fish to a plate, leaving the sauce in the pan.

Add the Chinese broccoli to the pan, and simmer until wilted and the sauce thickens slightly, about 4 minutes. Return the fish to the frying pan and heat through. Sprinkle with chopped cilantro and serve right away.

quick tips

Often, it's well worth the time and effort to make your own Asian-style curry paste, which comes together quickly in the food processor and keeps for at least 1 week in the refrigerator. This sauce is also great with scallops or chicken. If you can't find lemongrass at your local market, you can substitute 1 teaspoon finely grated lemon zest.

winter

Here, the simplest ingredients combine to make one of my favorite quick dinners: quickly sautéed pork medallions with sweet, nutty parsnips. I like to serve them with egg noodles tossed with olive oil, fresh thyme, and lots of fresh pepper.

sautéed pork with parsnips

Extra-virgin olive oil, 3 tablespoons

Parsnips, 10 oz (315 g), peeled and cut into ½-inch (12-mm) pieces

Shallots, 2, minced

Fresh thyme, 2 teaspoons plus 2½ tablespoons minced

Coarse kosher salt and freshly ground pepper

Wide egg noodles, 3 oz (90 g)

Pork tenderloin, 8–10 oz (250–315 g), cut crosswise into rounds ½ inch (12 mm) thick

All-purpose flour for dredging

Low-sodium chicken broth, 1 cup (8 fl oz/250 ml)

Dry vermouth, ½ cup (4 fl oz/125 ml)

makes 2 servings; can be doubled

● In a large nonstick frying pan over medium-high heat, warm 1 tablespoon of the oil. Add the parsnips and sauté for 2 minutes. Add the shallots and 2 teaspoons of the thyme. Sprinkle with salt and pepper and sauté until the parsnips start to brown, about 4 minutes. Transfer to a plate.

● Bring a large pot three-fourths full of salted water to a boil. Add the noodles, stir well, and cook until tender, about 7 minutes. Drain the noodles and return them to the same pot. Mix in 1 tablespoon of the oil and 1½ tablespoons of the thyme. Season to taste with salt and pepper. Cover to keep warm.

● Meanwhile, sprinkle the pork on both sides with salt and pepper. In the same frying pan used for the parsnips, warm the remaining 1 tablespoon oil over medium-high heat. Dredge the pork in the flour, shake off the excess, and add it to the frying pan. Cook until lightly browned, about 2½ minutes on each side. Transfer the pork to a plate.

● Add the broth, vermouth, and parsnip mixture to the frying pan and bring to a boil, stirring up the browned bits. Reduce the heat to medium and simmer, stirring occasionally, until the parsnips are tender, about 8 minutes. Add the pork and any juices from the plate. Simmer, turning the pork occasionally, until the pork is cooked through and the sauce thickens, about 2 minutes. Taste and adjust the seasoning. Sprinkle with the remaining 1 tablespoon thyme. Divide the pork between 2 plates and spoon the parsnips and sauce over the top. Divide the noodles between the plates and serve right away.

quick tips

The noodles could be replaced with rice or bulgur wheat, and carrots, sliced onions, rutabaga, or sweet potatoes could stand in for the parsnips. For a slightly sweet version, try dry sherry or Marsala in place of the vermouth.

This chili is deeply flavored with smoky chiles and fragrant ground spices. Accompany with cornbread or tortillas. For a light dessert, make extra of the yogurt-lime topping, sweeten it with brown sugar, and serve over fresh fruit.

chipotle-spiced **buffalo chili**

Olive oil, 1 tablespoon

Large onion, 1, chopped

Red bell peppers, 2, cut into ¾-inch (2-cm) pieces

Ground bison (buffalo) or ground beef, 1 lb (500 g)

Coarse kosher salt and freshly ground pepper

Ground dried chipotle chiles, 2 teaspoons

Ground cumin, 1 teaspoon

Ground cinnamon, ¼ teaspoon

Ground cloves, ⅛ teaspoon

Diced tomatoes, 2 cans (14.5 oz/455 g each)

Pinto or kidney beans, 2 cans (15 oz/470 g each), rinsed and drained

Dried oregano, 1 teaspoon

Plain yogurt, 1 cup (8 oz/250 g) (optional)

Grated lime zest, 2 teaspoons (optional)

makes 4–6 servings

● In a heavy large pot over medium-high heat, warm the oil. Add the onion and peppers and sauté until the onion is tender, about 10 minutes. Raise the heat to high, add the ground meat, and sprinkle with salt and pepper. Cook just until no longer red, breaking up the meat with a spoon, about 3 minutes. Add the ground chiles, cumin, cinnamon, and cloves, and stir until fragrant, about 2 minutes. Add the tomatoes with their juice, beans, oregano, and 1 cup (8 fl oz/250 ml) water. Cover and bring to a boil. Reduce the heat to medium-low and simmer until the flavors are blended, about 30 minutes.

● Meanwhile, if desired, mix the yogurt and lime zest in a small bowl.

● Taste the chili and adjust the seasoning. Spoon into warmed bowls. If using, spoon a dollop of lime-yogurt on top of each serving and serve right away.

quick tips

Look for ground bison, also called buffalo, at farmers' markets or natural food stores. The meat is lower in saturated fat, and higher in omega 3s than beef, but still has a rich flavor. Ground beef or turkey can replace the bison. This chili improves with reheating, so save extras for another meal.

winter

This innovative pasta dish starts with a quick shrimp and fennel stew, which I enhance with fragrant fennel seeds and shiny black kalamata olives. Start with a salad of purchased roasted red peppers, fresh mozzarella, and herbs.

pasta with fennel, tomatoes, olives, and shrimp

Olive oil, 1½ tablespoons

Fennel seeds, ½ teaspoon

Large fennel bulb, 1, cored and thinly sliced lengthwise, fronds chopped and reserved

Onion, 1, halved and thinly sliced

Red pepper flakes

Coarse kosher salt and freshly ground black pepper

Italian tomatoes, preferably San Marzano, 1 can (14.28 oz/448 g)

Pitted kalamata olives, ¼ cup (1 oz/30 g), quartered lengthwise

Dry white wine, 3 tablespoons

Shrimp, ½ lb (250 g), peeled and deveined

Spaghetti, preferably multigrain, 7–8 oz (220–250 g)

makes 2 servings; can be doubled

● Bring a large pot three-fourths full of salted water to a boil.

● Meanwhile, in a large frying pan over medium-high heat, warm the oil. Add the fennel seeds and stir until fragrant, about 10 seconds. Add the fennel bulb, onion, and a large pinch of red pepper flakes. Sprinkle with salt and black pepper. Sauté, stirring frequently, until the fennel and onion are tender and browning on the edges, about 10 minutes. Add the tomatoes, olives, and wine. Simmer, breaking up the tomatoes with a wooden spoon, until the sauce thickens, about 5 minutes. Add the shrimp and simmer until they are just opaque at the center, about 5 minutes; do not overcook.

● While the shrimp are cooking, add the pasta to the boiling water, stir well, and cook until al dente, about 11 minutes.

● Drain the pasta, add to the shrimp sauce, and stir to coat the pasta. Taste and adjust the seasoning and sprinkle with the fennel fronds. Transfer to a large warmed bowl and serve right away.

quick tips

To save time, I like to pick up roasted bell peppers and cheese packed in water from the deli on my way home from a busy day. Keep kalamata olives on hand in the refrigerator to add zest to salads and pastas. American shrimp are delicious and are a sustainable seafood choice.

winter

Here, sweet winter squash, earthy mushrooms, and woodsy fresh sage mingle in a warming meatless stew. The only accompaniment needed is crusty bread. For dessert, set out wheat meal biscuits, sliced pears, and a rich, creamy cheese.

white bean stew with porcini and winter squash

Dried porcini mushrooms, 2–2½ oz (60–75 g)

Olive oil, 1 tablespoon

Onions, 2, finely chopped

Serrano chiles, 2, seeded and minced

Fresh sage, 2 teaspoons minced

Butternut squash, 2 lb (1 kg), peeled, seeded, and cut into ½-inch (12-mm) pieces

Coarse kosher salt and freshly ground pepper

Cannellini beans, 2 cans (15 oz/470 g each) with liquid

Low-sodium vegetable or chicken broth, 2 cups (16 fl oz/500 ml)

Fresh flat-leaf parsley, chopped, for sprinkling

makes 4–6 servings

● Place the dried porcini in a sieve and rinse briefly with water. Transfer to a small bowl. Add 3 cups (24 fl oz/750 ml) very hot water and let soak until the mushrooms are softened, about 20 minutes.

● Meanwhile, in a heavy large pot over medium-high heat, warm the oil. Add the onions, chiles, and sage, and sauté until the onions are tender, about 8 minutes. Add the squash, season with salt and pepper, and sauté until it starts to soften, about 5 minutes. Add the beans with their liquid and the broth.

● Set a fine-mesh sieve over a small bowl. Drain the porcini in the sieve, pressing out as much liquid as possible from the mushrooms. Add the liquid to the pot. Chop the porcini and add to the pot. Simmer until the squash is tender and the flavors blend, about 20 minutes. Taste and adjust the seasoning. Spoon the stew into warmed bowls. Sprinkle with parsley and serve right away.

quick tips

For a heartier meal with extra protein, add sausage slices, chopped pancetta, a ham hock, or diced smoked turkey. If using the ham hock, simmer it whole in the stew, then remove the meat from the bone, chop it, and stir the chopped meat back into the stew. If you like, rosemary could replace the sage.

This sauce blends a medley of flavors—peppery ginger, fiery chiles, sweet brown sugar, tart vinegar, and toasty sesame oil—into a zesty sauce for fish. Serve the dish with brown rice and Chinese broccoli and spoon extra sauce over the rice.

roasted black cod with korean flavors

Olive oil, 1 tablespoon, plus more as needed

Large shallot, 1, minced

Fresh ginger, 2 teaspoons peeled and minced

Serrano chile, 1½ teaspoons minced

Low-sodium soy sauce, ⅓ cup (3 fl oz/80 ml)

Brown sugar, ¼ cup (2 oz/60 g) firmly packed

Rice vinegar, 3 tablespoons

Water, 3 tablespoons

Asian sesame oil, 1 tablespoon

Black cod fillets, 4 (about 6 oz/185 g each)

Green onions, 2, white and green parts, sliced

makes 4 servings

● Preheat the oven to 400°F (200°C).

● In a small saucepan over medium heat, warm the olive oil. Add the shallot, ginger, and chile, and sauté until tender, about 3 minutes. Add the soy sauce, sugar, vinegar, and water, and simmer until the mixture is reduced to ¾ cup (6 fl oz/180 ml), about 6 minutes. Remove from the heat and stir in the sesame oil. Set aside a small amount of the sauce for brushing.

● Brush a small baking pan with olive oil, and place the fish, skin side down, in the pan. Brush the fish with the reserved sauce. Roast until just cooked through, about 10 minutes. Transfer the fish to plates, sprinkle with green onions, and serve right away, passing the remaining sauce alongside.

quick tips

This Korean-style sauce takes only minutes to prepare, but adds a lot of flavor. I often make extra sauce and refrigerate the leftovers to use with roasted chicken or shrimp. It is also great stirred into rice or vegetables. The fish takes only 10 minutes to roast, so keep this dish in mind for an evening when you are pressed for time.

winter

Faster than a soup, but just as comforting, risotto takes only about 20 minutes to come together and is a favorite dish for weeknight dinners. Caramelized onions, cauliflower, and Parmesan cheese are a wonderful and unexpected combination.

cauliflower, onion, and greens **risotto**

Low-sodium chicken or vegetable broth, 4 cups (32 fl oz/1 l)

Olive oil, 1 tablespoon

Large onion, 1, coarsely chopped

Cauliflower, ½ head, cut into ½-inch (12-mm) florets

Arborio rice, 1½ cups (10½ oz/330 g)

Dry white wine, ½ cup (4 fl oz/125 ml)

Beet greens or other greens, 1 bunch, stems removed, and leaves thinly sliced

Parmesan cheese, 1 cup (¼ lb/125 g) freshly grated

Fresh marjoram, 1½ tablespoons minced

Coarse kosher salt and freshly ground pepper

makes 4 servings

● In a small saucepan over high heat, bring the broth and 1 cup (8 fl oz/250 ml) water to a boil. Reduce the heat to low and keep the liquid hot.

● In a heavy large saucepan over medium-high heat, warm the oil. Add the onion and sauté until golden, about 8 minutes. Add the cauliflower and sauté until heated through, about 2 minutes. Add the rice and sauté until opaque, about 1 minute. Pour in the wine and stir until absorbed, about 2 minutes. Add about ¾ cup (6 fl oz/180 ml) of the hot broth, reduce the heat so the broth simmers slowly, and cook until absorbed, stirring frequently. Continue cooking, adding the broth by about ¾ cup at a time and stirring frequently until the rice is not quite tender, but still slightly firm, about 15 minutes.

● Add the greens and continue cooking, stirring almost constantly, adding the liquid about ½ cup (4 fl oz/125 ml) at a time, until the rice is just tender but slightly firm in the center and the mixture is creamy, about 5 minutes longer. Remove the risotto from the heat. Stir in the cheese and the marjoram. Season to taste with salt and a generous amount of pepper. Spoon the risotto into warmed bowls and serve right away.

quick tips

Greens add great nutrition and health experts recommend that we should eat them every day, so I sneak them into my cooking wherever I can. Shiny beet greens add a fresh flavor and an intriguing pink tint to this risotto, but any cooking greens would be delicious. If whole beets come along with the greens, wrap them in foil, roast them while making dinner, and then turn them into a salad for another day.

I love the full flavor of beef triangle, or tri-tip, roast—a very popular cut in California. Here, I season the meat with a blend of spices, herbs, and spicy mustard. To round out the plate, roast small potatoes at the same time.

tri-tip roast with brussels sprouts and shallots

Tri-tip beef roast, 1¾–2 lb (875 g–1 kg), most of fat layer trimmed

Coarse kosher salt and freshly ground black pepper

Sweet paprika, 2¼ teaspoons

Caraway seeds, 2 teaspoons

Dried marjoram, 2 teaspoons

Dry mustard, 1 teaspoon

Cayenne pepper, ½ teaspoon

Olive oil, 3½ tablespoons, plus more for greasing

Brussels sprouts, 1 lb (500 g), cut in half lengthwise

Small shallots, ¾ lb (375 g), halved lengthwise, plus 1 large shallot, minced

Low-sodium soy sauce, 1 tablespoon, plus 2 teaspoons

Dry vermouth, ½ cup (4 fl oz/125 ml)

Low-sodium beef or chicken broth, ½ cup (4 fl oz/125 ml)

Unsalted butter, 2 teaspoons

makes 4–6 servings

● Place one rack in the center and one rack in the lower third of the oven; preheat to 450°F (230°C). Season the beef all over with salt and pepper, and place on a baking rack set in a shallow roasting pan.

● In a small bowl, combine 2 teaspoons of the paprika, 1 teaspoon of the caraway seeds, ½ teaspoon of the marjoram, and the mustard and cayenne. Mix in 1 tablespoon of the oil. Spread the mixture on both sides of the beef. Brush a 9-by-13-inch (23-by-33-cm) baking pan with olive oil; add the brussels sprouts, halved shallots, remaining 2½ tablespoons oil, the 1 tablespoon soy sauce, remaining 1 teaspoon caraway seeds, and 1 teaspoon of the marjoram, and mix to coat. Place pan with the beef on the center oven rack, and place the pan with the vegetables on the lower rack. Roast the beef until an instant-read thermometer inserted in the thickest part registers 120°F (49°C) for rare, about 20 minutes, or until cooked to your liking. Roast the vegetables until tender and they begin to brown, about 25 minutes. Remove the beef from the oven and transfer to a warmed platter. Cover loosely with foil and let rest 15 minutes.

● Spoon 1 tablespoon of the fat from the beef roasting pan into a heavy saucepan; discard the remaining fat. Heat the saucepan over medium heat. Add the minced shallot and sauté until it begins to soften, about 1 minute. Meanwhile, add the vermouth to the roasting pan, set the pan over medium-high heat, and bring to a boil, stirring up the browned bits on the pan bottom. Pour the mixture into the saucepan and boil until syrupy, about 3 minutes. Add the broth, remaining ¼ teaspoon paprika, and the 2 teaspoons soy sauce to the pan. Boil the sauce until syrupy, about 5 minutes.

● Remove the saucepan from the heat. Pour in any beef juices from the platter. Whisk in the butter and the remaining ½ teaspoon marjoram. Season the sauce to taste with salt and black pepper. Slice the beef and arrange on a warmed platter with the vegetables. Serve right away with the sauce.

plan ahead for fresh & fast meals

Having on hand a good supply of pantry staples will provide a solid foundation for putting together quick meals throughout the week. If your cupboard is well stocked with such things as dried pastas and grains, canned beans and tomatoes, a good supply of oils and vinegars, prepared broths, and flavorful spices, you should only need to shop a couple times a week for perishable ingredients, such as fresh produce, meat, poultry, or seafood. If you know that you'll be pressed for time during the week, try to plan your meals ahead of time and purchase your meat, poultry, and fish on the weekend. Once you get home, wrap, label, and freeze what you won't be using within the next couple of days; remember to move the frozen items to the refrigerator to thaw on the night before you will need them.

pantry checklist

Below is a list of basic kitchen staples that are used in many of the recipes in this book. Keep a supply of the following items on hand to help make tempting meals any time of the year.

flavorings

- ☐ Asian chile sauce such as sriracha or sambal oelek
- ☐ Assorted spices
- ☐ Capers
- ☐ Dijon mustard
- ☐ Dried herbs
- ☐ Dried porcini mushrooms
- ☐ Kalamata olives
- ☐ Tomato paste in a tube
- ☐ Wasabi paste

liquid flavorings

- ☐ Asian fish sauce
- ☐ Clam juice
- ☐ Dry white wine or vermouth
- ☐ Low-sodium organic broth: chicken, beef, vegetable
- ☐ Low-sodium soy sauce
- ☐ Pomegranate molasses
- ☐ Vinegar: balsamic, red wine, rice, sherry, white wine

vegetables and legumes

- ☐ Canned beans: black, cannellini, chickpeas
- ☐ Canned tomatoes: diced, fire-roasted, San Marzano
- ☐ Dried brown lentils

oils

- ☐ Asian sesame oil
- ☐ Olive oil: regular and extra-virgin
- ☐ Vegetable oil such as peanut or grape seed

starches & grains

- ☐ Arborio rice
- ☐ Brown basmati or jasmine rice
- ☐ Bulgur wheat, quick cooking
- ☐ Couscous, quick cooking
- ☐ Egg noodles
- ☐ Dried ribbon pasta: fettuccine, pappardelle
- ☐ Multigrain pasta such as Barilla Plus
- ☐ Orzo
- ☐ Polenta
- ☐ Quinoa

miscellaneous

- ☐ All-purpose flour
- ☐ Panko (Japanese bread crumbs)

quick tips for fresh & fast meals

For me, dinner planning starts with the raw ingredients: I let what's fresh and in season be the star of my meals. But once I decide on a dish, a handful of smart strategies, such as those that follow, help ensure I can get a delicious meal on the table in minutes.

cook with the seasons Keep the weather in mind when shopping. On a hot day you might opt for a quick, no-cook salad or dinner grilled al fresco; on a cool day, a comforting braise or warm, oven-roasted meal would feel more appropriate.

shop smart When shopping, keep your eye out for vegetables that can be simply prepared—steamed, sautéed, roasted—to accompany seasonal meals.

plan ahead Assemble and measure all of your ingredients before you begin cooking. That way, you won't need to search for ingredients at the last minute, and the kitchen won't be cluttered.

minimize equipment Aim to use as few pans as possible when preparing meals. Not only does this streamline the cooking process, but also it saves time in cleanup.

time it right Keep quick-cooking couscous in the cupboard; it takes only 5 minutes to steam. Or, put rice on to cook before starting dinner preparations; it will be ready to serve when the entrée is finished.

be creative Re-think what's appropriate for dinner. Some of the most popular suppers in my house include items that you might normally think of as breakfast or lunch foods; for example, egg dishes, tacos, sandwiches, and pizzas are favorites.

top it off Consider cold sauces, such as salsas, pestos, raitas, and vinaigrettes. These versatile mixtures can often be made ahead of time—and in large batches—and to be used with tonight's meal as well as others during the week.

kitchen tools checklist

In addition to a good set of knives and a cutting board, you'll need only a few key tools and minimal equipment to prepare fresh and fast meals.

basic tools

- ☐ Bowls in assorted sizes
- ☐ Colander and sieve
- ☐ Instant-read thermometer
- ☐ Rasp grater
- ☐ Salad spinner
- ☐ Small prep bowls for ingredients

specialty tools

- ☐ Charcoal or gas grill
- ☐ Meat mallet or rolling pin
- ☐ Poultry shears
- ☐ Steamer or steamer insert

kitchen electrics

- ☐ Food processor
- ☐ Spice mill or mortar & pestle

pots and pans

- ☐ Broiler pan or stove-top grill pan
- ☐ Dutch oven
- ☐ Glass baking dish, small
- ☐ Large pot for pasta, soup, or stew
- ☐ Metal baking pans
- ☐ Nonstick frying pans, medium & large
- ☐ Ovenproof frying pans, small & medium
- ☐ Rimmed baking sheets, large & small
- ☐ Rimless baking sheet or pizza pan
- ☐ Saucepans, small, medium & large

fresh foods for quick weeknight meals

When planning fresh and fast dinners, I start with the fresh produce I find at the farmers market, and let it inspire the other ingredients—such as meat, poultry, or fish—in the meal. The same rules apply for buying these ingredients as for fruits and vegetables: I purchase the very best I can find. For the most delicious meals, seek out a butcher, fishmonger, or dairy specialist that stocks top-notch ingredients at reasonable prices, and patronize them regularly.

chicken and turkey I choose organic poultry whenever possible, as I believe it to have the best flavor and be the most wholesome choice. When I'm in a hurry, I buy pieces that are ready to cook: among my favorites are boneless, skinless chicken breast halves; chicken breast tenders; and boneless, skinless chicken thighs. Cut from the breast meat and flattened, chicken and turkey cutlets are a wonderful choice for quick sautés. When choosing ground turkey for burgers or stews, I favor dark meat, or a mixture of white and dark meat, as it lends more flavor and moisture to a dish than does ground breast meat.

beef Try grass-fed beef from humanely raised animals for better nutrition—it's a sound option for healthy weeknight meals. For everyday cooking, I choose beef cuts that are trim and economical: Top sirloin or top round works well for salads and stir-fries; tri-tip is a good choice for roasting or can be cut into medallions for sautéing; and flank and skirt steak are great for grilling and cutting into kabobs.

bison Also called buffalo, bison meat is leaner than beef and high in omega-3 fatty acids, which contribute to a healthy diet. Bison's recent popularity has made it more available than ever at the meat counter in natural- or specialty-food stores, quality butcher shops, as well as some farmers markets. I like to use ground bison in burgers and chilis to help keep weeknight dinners lean, flavorful, and wholesome.

lamb Naturally lean lamb is a terrific alternative to beef, and can lend its unique flavor to give weeknight meals a fresh twist. In the summer, I like to sauté or grill round-bone shoulder chops or loin or rib chops and top them with a quick fruit relish or herb sauce. Boneless leg of lamb (buy it already boned from your butcher) is delicious roasted or grilled or turned into kabobs. Ground lamb enlivens everyday burgers and pasta sauces.

pork Like beef, today's pork is leaner than ever and is a fine choice for healthful dinners. For weeknight meals, pork tenderloin is a versatile choice, as it can be roasted whole or cut into medallions and sautéed. When seared, center-cut pork chops give steak-like appeal for less money than beef. And when I'm in the mood for ribs but not for their typical long cooking times, baby back ribs are the perfect choice. For the best flavor and humane treatment, I choose pork that has been raised on a small family farm. Another pork product I always keep on hand is pancetta, a type of unsmoked, Italian-style bacon. Just a little bit of pancetta goes a long way to flavor and lend substance to a variety of dishes.

sausages There are a number of high-quality sausages on the market today, including andouille and Italian-style sausages, that are made from chicken and turkey. Used cleverly in pizzas, risottos, pastas, stews, and similar dishes, these poultry sausages can lend surprising depth without the higher quantity of fat that is typical of sausages made from ground pork.

seafood Fish fillets and steaks and all kinds of shellfish are mainstays of my cooking repertory, as they cook so quickly and are healthy choices. I am passionate about using only sustainable seafood, which is reflected in these recipes. My current favorite fish include albacore tuna, black cod, halibut, mahi mahi, tilapia, and wild king salmon. For shellfish, I enjoy wild American shrimp, sea scallops, Manila clams, and mussels. To learn more about sustainable seafood, and discover the best seafood choices for cooking, visit montereybayaquarium.org and click on the Seafood Watch link.

cheese For cooking, I favor bold-flavored cheeses and use them moderately. My favorites include soft, fresh goat cheese and ricotta; semifirm Cheddar, Comté (a type of Gruyère), and manchego for melting; crumbly feta and blue cheese for salads, risottos, and pastas; and firm grating cheeses like Parmesan (preferably authentic Parmigiano-Reggiano) and pecorino romano.

eggs Many farmers' markets offer fresh, recently gathered eggs. I like the deep-orange color of the yolks and the satisfaction I get from buying from a local farm. An overlooked choice for dinner, eggs are one of the best quick-cooking ingredients for weeknight meals. I use them to make frittatas, soufflés, and fritters, as well as to perch atop flavorful vegetable ragouts.

tofu From time to time, protein-rich tofu makes a welcome appearance in my recipes. I love how well it soaks up the flavor of the ingredients cooked with it and its meaty, satisfying texture. Tofu comes in varying densities, but I usually buy firm style. It is solid enough to hold its shape while cooking, yet still moist in the center. Sold packed in water or in aseptic packaging, tofu should be drained, rinsed, and then drained again before use.

making the most of your meals

In my house, "leftovers" is not a dirty word. In fact, the meals eaten on subsequent days are often some of my favorites, thanks to their deepened and well-integrated flavors. The best feature of this make-more-to-store philosophy is knowing that a home-cooked dinner is waiting for me when I return home from a busy day. Listed below are some of my favorite strategies for creating—and using—leftovers.

think ahead Since my schedule is so full, I've started the habit of imagining new meals I can make with the leftovers of tonight's dinner. Fortunately, because my pantry is well stocked, and my time is well organized, this task is never daunting.

cook on the weekend On Saturdays and Sundays, when I tend to spend more leisurely time in the kitchen, I might roast an extra chicken or grill an extra steak or two to turn into hearty salads, sandwiches, or pasta dishes for an upcoming night.

aim for extras My household consists of just two people, but I'll often make recipes that serve four with the intention of having leftovers. Tossed with cooked rice, bulgur, or pasta, and flavored with a bold vinaigrette or simple sauce, these dishes become welcome treats on subsequent nights.

simmer your supper I love to turn leftovers into a hearty soup: Sauté a chopped onion, add a couple of cans of drained beans—cannellini, black, or kidney—and broth, then whatever leftover vegetables, meat, or poultry are in the refrigerator.

fold and serve Almost any leftovers make great taco fillings: Cut meat, poultry, fish, or vegetables into bite-size pieces and heat through in a frying pan. Serve with warmed tortillas and purchased salsa. In summer, make a quick salsa by chopping tomatoes, onion, chile, and a fresh herb; mix in a squeeze of fresh lime juice.

tips for storing leftovers

Following are seven simple tips to ensure your leftovers stay fresh and wholesome and will become delicious meals in their own right.

- Store slightly cooked leftovers in an airtight container in the refrigerator for up to 4 days or in the freezer for up to 4 months.

- Freeze food in small batches, which allows you to heat up just enough to serve one or two people.

- Clearly label items for freezing with the dish name and date they were made. Remember to move them to the refrigerator a day before eating so they can be reheated quickly.

- Be sure to thaw frozen foods in the refrigerator or in the microwave (to avoid bacterial contamination); never thaw them at room temperature.

- Don't crowd foods in the refrigerator or freezer. Air should circulate freely to keep foods evenly cooled.

- Check the contents of the refrigerator at least once a week and promptly discard old or spoiled food.

- Let food cool slightly before refrigerating, then chill before freezing. Transfer the cooled food to an airtight plastic or glass container, leaving room for expansion if freezing.

basic recipes

Following are a handful of recipes for healthy grains and starchy vegetables that can round out meals.

pizza dough

Active dry yeast,
1 tablespoon

Warm water (110°F/43°C),
¾ cup plus 2 tablespoons
(7 fl oz/210 ml)

Extra-virgin olive oil,
1 tablespoon

All-purpose flour,
2¾ cups (14 oz/440 g)

Salt, 1 teaspoon

makes 1 lb (500 g) dough

● In the bowl of a stand mixer, sprinkle the yeast over the warm water and let stand until foamy, about 5 minutes. Place the bowl on the mixer fitted with the dough hook and add the olive oil, ½ cup (2½ oz/75 g) of the flour, and salt; mix until combined. Add the remaining flour, ½ cup at a time, and knead with the dough hook until the dough is smooth but not sticky, about 10 minutes.

● Remove the dough from the mixer, form into a ball, and place in an oiled bowl, turning to coat all sides. Cover the bowl with plastic wrap and let the dough rise in a warm place until doubled in volume, 1–2 hours.

● To shape the dough, turn it out onto a lightly floured work surface and press flat. Using your hands, begin to press it out gently and then pull, stretch, or roll the dough into the desired shape and thickness, usually about 12 inches (30 cm) in diameter and about ¼ inch (6 mm) thick. Flipping the dough over from time to time as you work with it.

saffron rice

Olive oil, 1 tablespoon

Shallot, 1 small, chopped

Basmati rice, 1 cup

Coarse kosher salt

Saffron threads,
¼ teaspoon, crumbled

makes 4–5 servings

● In a saucepan, warm the oil over medium-high heat. Add the shallot and sauté until translucent, about 2 minutes. Add the rice, 2 cups (16 fl oz/500 ml) water, ½ teaspoon salt, and the saffron and bring to a boil. Reduce the heat to low, cover, and simmer for about 20 minutes.

● Fluff the rice with a fork and serve right away.

brown aromatic rice

Brown basmati or jasmine rice,
1⅓ cups (9½ oz/295 g)

makes 4–6 servings

● In a saucepan, bring 2 cups (16 fl oz/500 ml) salted water to a boil over high heat. Add the rice and return to a boil. Reduce the heat to low, cover, and cook for 30 minutes.

● Keep the pan covered, turn off the heat and let stand 5 minutes. Fluff the rice with a fork and serve right away.

basic cooked quinoa

Quinoa, 1 cup (6 oz/185 g)

**Coarse kosher salt and
freshly ground pepper**

Olive oil, 2 teaspoons

makes 4–6 servings

● Place the quinoa in a sieve and rinse well under cold running water.

● In a saucepan, bring 2 cups (16 fl oz/500 ml) water to a boil over high heat. Add the rinsed quinoa and ½ teaspoon salt. Reduce the heat to low, cover, and simmer until the water is absorbed and the grain is tender, about 20 minutes.

● Drizzle the cooked quinoa with olive oil, season to taste with salt and pepper, and toss well with a fork. Serve right away.

basic cooked bulgur

Bulgur wheat, quick cooking,
1 cup (6 oz/185 g)

Coarse kosher salt

makes 4–6 servings

● In a saucepan, combine the bulgur and 1½ cups (12 fl oz/375 ml) cold water. Sprinkle lightly with salt. Bring the water to a boil over high heat. Reduce the heat to low, cover, and simmer until the bulgur is just tender, 12–15 minutes. Turn off the heat and let the bulgur stand, covered, for at least 5 minutes.

● Fluff the bulgur with a fork and serve right away.

basic cooked couscous

Broth or water, 1 cup (8 fl oz/250 ml)

Olive oil, 1 teaspoon

Coarse kosher salt and freshly ground pepper

Quick-cooking couscous, 1 cup

makes 4–6 servings

● In a heavy saucepan over medium heat, bring the broth to a boil over high heat. Add the olive oil and ½ teaspoon salt.

● Stir in the couscous, remove from the heat, cover the pan, and let stand for 5 minutes. Fluff the grains with a fork, season to taste, and serve.

herbed polenta

Olive oil, 1 tablespoon

Small onion, ½, chopped

Coarse kosher salt and freshly ground pepper

Polenta, 1 cup (7 oz/220 g)

Fresh marjoram or thyme, 1 tablespoon chopped

Parmesan or romano cheese, ¾ cup (3 oz/90 g) coarsely grated

makes 4–6 servings

● In a heavy saucepan over medium heat, warm the oil. Add the onion and sauté until tender, about 5 minutes. Add 4 cups (32 fl oz/1 l) water, 1 teaspoon salt, and 1 teaspoon pepper and bring to a boil over high heat.

● Gradually whisk in the polenta. Bring the mixture back to a boil, stirring frequently. Reduce the heat to low and simmer slowly, stirring frequently, until the polenta is thick, about 18 minutes.

● Mix in the cheese and marjoram and serve right away.

olive oil–mashed potatoes

Yukon gold potatoes, 2 lb (1 kg), peeled

Coarse kosher salt and freshly ground pepper

Milk, 1 cup (8 fl oz/250 ml)

Extra-virgin olive oil, 3 tablespoons

makes 4–6 servings

● Put the potatoes in a large saucepan and add water to cover by 1 inch (2.5 cm). Add 1 teaspoon salt, place over high heat, and bring the water to a boil. Reduce the heat to low and simmer until the potatoes are tender when pierced with a knife, 25–30 minutes.

● In a small saucepan, warm the milk over medium heat until small bubbles form around the edges of the pan. Remove from the heat and stir in the olive oil.

● Drain the potatoes and return to the pot. Using a potato masher, mash the potatoes until smooth. Using a wooden spoon, gently mix in the milk-oil mixture. Season to taste with salt and pepper and serve right away.

index

236

weldonowen

415 Jackson Street, Suite 200, San Francisco, CA 94111
Telephone: 415 291 0100 Fax: 415 291 8841
www.wopublishing.com

Weldon Owen is a division of
BONNIER

WILLIAMS-SONOMA, INC.
Founder and Vice-Chairman Chuck Williams

WELDON OWEN, INC.
CEO and President Terry Newell
VP, Sales and Marketing Amy Kaneko
Director of Finance Mark Perrigo

VP and Publisher Hannah Rahill
Executive Editor Jennifer Newens
Editor Donita Boles
Assistant Editor Becky Duffett

Associate Creative Director Emma Boys
Art Director Alexandra Zeigler
Associate Art Director Diana Heom

Production Director Chris Hemesath
Production Manager Michelle Duggan
Color Manager Teri Bell

Photographer Kate Sears
Food Stylist Lori Powell
Prop Stylist Christine Wolheim

WEEKNIGHT FRESH & FAST
Conceived and produced by Weldon Owen, Inc.
In collaboration with Williams-Sonoma, Inc.
3250 Van Ness Avenue, San Francisco, CA 94109

A WELDON OWEN PRODUCTION
Copyright © 2011 Weldon Owen, Inc. and Williams-Sonoma, Inc.
All rights reserved, including the right of reproduction
in whole or in part in any form.

Color separations by Embassy Graphics in Canada
Printed and bound by Toppan Leefung Printing Limited in China

First printed in 2010
10 9 8 7 6 5 4 3 2 1

Library of Congress Control Number: 2010937207

ISBN13: 978-1-61628-057-4
ISBN 10: 1-61628-057-3

ACKNOWLEDGMENTS
Weldon Owen wishes to thank the following people for their generous support in producing this book:
T. Shane Gilman, Julia Humes, Kim Laidlaw, Lesli Nielson, Elizabeth Parson, Karen Seriguchi, Victoria Wall, and Jason Wheeler